THE SEED SOWER

A 40-Day Journey
to Sow Seed & Harvest Fruit

Tammy L. Jordan

THE SEED SOWER
A 40-Day Journey to Sow Seed & Harvest Fruit

By Tammy L. Jordan
Copyright @ 2013 ShadeTree Publishing, LLC
Print ISBN: 978-1-937331-53-5
e-Book ISBN: 978-1-937331-54-2
Cover photography by Steve Brightwell

All Bible Verses are from KJV Blue Letter Bible online.

The purpose of this book is to educate and enlighten. This book is sold with the understanding that the author and publisher are not engaged in rendering counseling, albeit it professional or lay, to the reader or anyone else. The author and publisher shall have neither liability nor responsibility to any person or entity with respect to any loss or damage caused, or alleged to have been caused, directly or indirectly, by the information contained in this book. The information in this book does not necessarily reflect the opinion of the publisher.

Visit our Web site at www.ShadeTreePublishing.com

In Memory of:

Sue Scott, my dear friend and co-laborer in Christ. She generously scattered seeds of God's hope into the lives of all those around her, especially during her long and difficult battle with cancer. She was unconcerned that she may never reap these seeds herself.

Sue deeply planted encouragement, unity, and hope into my life, as we labored together for years with the church choir.

Her last week on earth, she was sowing seeds of rest into her own life, so she could come and support this ministry by attending the opening celebration of Fruits of Labor Training and Retreat Center. Instead of visiting the mountaintop at the Retreat Center, God gave her a greater mountaintop experience. He called her home to Heaven.

Sue is greatly missed, but the seeds she planted into the lives of those around her are growing and bearing fruit. This continued harvest stands as a testimony to her labors. "both he that soweth and he that reapeth may rejoice together." John 4:36

Table of Contents

Sow to yourselves in righteousness, reap in mercy; break up your fallow ground: for [it is] *time to seek the LORD, till he come and rain righteousness upon you.*

-Hosea 10:12

Introduction

At some point in our walk with the Lord, we often feel a strong desire to harvest First Fruits for Christ and experience more fruitful results in our Christian life.

To have a beautiful garden ready for harvest in the summer, we must be willing to plant many seeds in the spring. The same concept is true of our Christian walk. We will never harvest a bounty of First Fruits, if we fail to plant many seeds along life's way.

Now is the time to start sowing seeds! Embark on this forty-day journey as a seed sower and explore different types of seeds including physical, mental, emotional, spiritual, and wholeness ones.

This book includes forty different seeds that are vital ingredients for a fruitful walk with God. You will examine each seed, and learn why it is important and how to sow it. In *Sowing the Seeds*, you will be challenged to grow as a sower and instructed in the ways God uses to prepare you for His harvest. In *Seeds of Change Prayer*, you will ask God to help you be a more effective sower and harvester in His Kingdom. Lastly, in *First Fruits*, you will record how God is instructing you to sow that particular seed and list what fruit it produces.

On this journey, learn to scatter the seeds of God's truth, and He will give the increase. In time, hope will bloom in your life and the lives of others around you, as you gather fruit from the sowing efforts.

Tammy L Jordan

Part One: Physical Seeds

Service
Perseverance
Purity
Charity
Provision
Temperance
Strength
Rest

Tammy L Jordan

Day 1: Sow Seeds of Service

*And let us not be weary in well doing: for in due
season we shall reap, if we faint not.*

-Galatians 6:9

It is easy to become distracted and weary in our daily
walk. Often, we refuse to set aside time devoted to service for
our Lord. So many external things rob us of this valuable
experience with Him. These things may be good, wholesome
activities, but they can get us off track with what God has
planned for our future. It is important to pause at different
intervals to take inventory of life and review how we spend our
short time here on earth. During this time of being still and
seeking direction, we need to enlist the help of the Father to
show us the next step. We must learn to listen with open
minds and hearts, and remain willing to follow Him. When
deciding whether to follow His leading, we should remember
that our life is no longer our own. Christ purchased us with
His blood, and we glorify Him by being His servants.

We must not be weary servants, but rather be cheerful
givers to others. How do we not become weary in well doing?
The first step is by allowing our Father to mend and tend to our
hearts completely. He desires our wholeness. When we run in
our own strength, we eventually run to a place of emptiness.
He wants to fill us first with His strength and then let us sow in
His strength, and not our own. Without seeking the Master
Gardener's plan for healthy sowing and reaping, this experience
of seed sowing will be more exhausting than hope producing.
We must come to God empty and let Him fill us with His ways,
His strength, and His plan. It is necessary to expose our often
hidden wounds so that He may first bring healing to our mind,
body, soul, and spirit. The Lord understands that sowing seeds
is about sowing a part of ourselves with each experience. We
have a finite supply of pieces of our life, but when we follow His
plan we are not limited by our supply, we pull from the infinite
supply of God's storehouse.

Sowing the Seeds

Let God have your life today to tend, heal, and then fill. Place your whole life before Him, and He will lovingly review each part. He will bind up your wounds, replace your fears with trust, and give you peace to embrace the plans of the day. As you grow in this lifestyle change, God will be able to use you effectively as a seed sower, directed by His leading and running at His pace. You will learn that when you follow God and are willing to wait on His timing, He will prompt you when and how to serve. On the journey, you will start to view others as God sees them. As you sow in His strength, you shall reap the rewards of seeing Christ call others to Him through your labors. Sow with joy. Do not faint in the labors of faith. In time, the season of harvesting First Fruits will arrive.

Seeds of Change Prayer

God, please let me not become weary in doing Your work. Show me the needs of others as You see them. Guide me to change my path of normal, to a journey in Your service. Through that service, may I be transformed so that others see only You working through me!

First Fruits

Record how God is instructing you to sow Seeds of Service
and list what fruit it produces.

_____

_____

_____

_____

_____

_____

_____

_____

_____

_____

_____

_____

_____

_____

_____

_____

_____

And let us not be weary in well doing: for in due season we shall reap, if we faint not.
-Galatians 6:9

Day 2: Sow Seeds of Perseverance

Wait on the LORD: be of good courage, and he shall strengthen thine heart: wait, I say, on the LORD.

-Psalms 27:14

In gardening, we spend most of the season waiting for the time of reaping; however, there is much to do while awaiting the harvest. If the farmer quits before the fruit has matured, weeds and disease will consume any hope of a harvest from that year's planting. The same is true with our journey in life.

Everyone is usually waiting on something. What are you waiting on today? Are you waiting on healing, financial security, a new job, or a restored marriage? During times of waiting, we often grow discouraged. Unwilling to continue our labors in the middle of this season, we find ourselves at a crossroads of either moving forward or quitting and allowing the weeds of life to choke our hope. In the midst of exhaustion, we may simply sit down on the side of the road and make a conscience decision to stop.

To persevere in times of struggles and trials is a difficult task, but necessary for continued growth and development as a Christian. Waiting for an unknown length of time or outcome can easily become a place of discouragement. However, we have biblical direction on the subject of perseverance. We are encouraged not only to wait in times of drought, but also to be of good courage while we wait. In other words, we are to press forward in the direction God leads regardless of our current circumstances. He promises to strengthen our hearts during a season of perseverance.

Sowing the Seeds

Each one of us, at some point, has crossed the path of others who are discouraged and ready to give up. This hurting and 'open ground' is the place we are called to sow seeds of perseverance into their life. Take time to show someone the great joy that results in the willingness to continue to persevere, and become that physical reminder that God will strengthen their heart during this season of waiting. God is not finished with His work in their life.

Seeds of Change Prayer

Lord, give me the grace needed to persevere in times of trials. Let me stand in Your strength alone, so that others will see a difference in my life. May this change in me be a testimony to Your great power, and an encouragement to those who are facing the choice to continue forward or to stop in the midst of discouragement.

First Fruits

Record how God is instructing you to sow Seeds of
Perseverance
and list what fruit it produces.

_____

_____

_____

_____

_____

_____

_____

_____

_____

_____

_____

_____

_____

_____

*Wait on the LORD: be of good courage, and he shall strengthen thine heart: wait,
I say, on the LORD.*
-Psalms 27:14

Day 3: Sow Seeds of Purity

Let no man despise thy youth; but be thou an example of the believers, in word, in conversation, in charity, in spirit, in faith, in purity.

I Timothy 4:12

Purity is a difficult trait to protect. However, without protecting purity, our identity as a Christian swiftly blends with the world's identity. Sometimes in the field of agriculture, we wish to keep the genetic line pure of a certain variety of plant; therefore, we must grow them away from certain other plant types. Setting two kinds of tomatoes in different fields will keep them from cross-pollinating with each other. Cross-pollination will forever change the purity of the seeds produced from those plants, and may often yield undesirable and unpredictable results.

The Bible challenges us to be set apart from worldly ways. It is also important to note there is great encouragement to draw away from the world's clutches and draw close to the Heavenly Father's ways during youth. When we embrace the way of our Savior early in life, we have an opportunity to be a light of Christ for a greater length of time.

Remaining pure is not limited to just purity of the body, but also in word, conversation, and our love toward one another. Purity also spills over into the spiritual side of our life. We need our motives to remain pure, as well as our faith. This path of purity is not a popular path in today's society; however, when we decide to set aside our life and live a life of purity, God can use us an example to other believers.

Sowing the Seeds

Purity comes in many forms. Society tends to focus on physical purity but spiritual purity is often harder to maintain. Think about your spiritual life. Are you volunteering because there is something in it for you? (In other words, are your motives pure?) Do your conversations convey the love you profess to have for fellow believers or are your words tainted when you find yourself among gossipers? As you sow seeds of purity, God will bring other believers in your path. Take the time to develop relationships with these individuals so they can see the fruit of purity in your life.

Seeds of Change Prayer

Lord, I desire to be a vessel that You use to shine Your light to those around me. I know that in order to become that type of vessel, I must be willing to set aside the world and embrace the purity of Your ways. I am willing to pay the cost. I also understand that it is never too late in life to allow You to show me how to draw away from the world and to begin living in ways of purity. Please help me to sow seeds of purity into others by example, so they will also experience the great results You have planned.

First Fruits

Record how God is instructing you to sow Seeds of Purity
and list what fruit it produces.

_____

_____

_____

_____

_____

_____

_____

_____

_____

_____

_____

_____

_____

_____

_____

_____

_____

*Let no man despise thy youth; but be thou an example of the believers, in word,
in conversation, in charity, in spirit, in faith, in purity.*
-1 Timothy 4:12

Day 4: Sow Seeds of Charity

And now abideth faith, hope, charity, these three;
but the greatest of these [is] *charity.*
1Corinthians 13:13

"Faith, hope, charity...the greatest is charity." We've heard this verse so many times. More often than not, the minister uses these words during a wedding ceremony to remind the bride and groom that charity (or love) is the greatest of all.

Sometimes we fall prey to the concept of loving in word, but not loving in deed. Today, we are challenged to sow seeds of charity, not only in the lives of our family and close friends, but also to those who are strangers. An act of benevolence towards an individual or group of people who may never know you or be able to repay the kindness can produce amazing results.

The Fruits of Labor Training & Retreat Center grows produce to help supply its agricultural needs. Most years, harvest time produces abundance far beyond its need. A couple of years ago through a divine appointment on a plane trip, God allowed the owner (namely, me) to sit beside a man from my hometown. His wife worked at the local homeless shelter, and we began a discussion about it. One thing led to another, and the topic of nutritious food came up. He needed food for the homeless shelter, and we had extra produce that could help. Our seed sown that spring turned into needed produce for the homeless shelter later that summer.

The next year, the students in the local culinary program needed additional practice with knife skills on fresh produce, but the cost was too great. We took our extra produce to them. They learned about different varieties of local produce, washed it, practiced knife skills, packed the prepared produce, and delivered it to the local homeless shelter ready to use. I later met with the teacher of the program to discuss whether the students would like to continue the program. She said yes and shared that the class had prepared food each month through the winter for the homeless shelter. It is amazing to watch a planted seed take root, and then grow far beyond the initial seed.

Sowing the Seeds

Find a practical way to sow a seed of charity. Keep your eyes open for an opportunity to serve in your community. Charity comes in many forms. Do not be surprised if God asks you to do something outside your comfort zone. Give something you have never given and do something you have never done before. Be prepared to donate your time, your talent, and your resources as you sow a seed of charity that will produce fruit beyond your wildest imagination.

Seeds of Change Prayer

Lord, please help me change the way I love others. Please help me to refrain from loving with just words, but help me also love in deed. I understand this change may cost me in effort, resources, and time. Let me not hold too tightly to the things of this world, but allow Your blessings to transfer through me to others as You reveal their needs. Let the way that I love be more reflective of the way You love me!

First Fruits

Record how God is instructing you to sow Seeds of Charity
and list what fruit it produces.

_____

_____

_____

_____

_____

_____

_____

_____

_____

_____

_____

_____

_____

_____

_____

*And now abideth faith, hope, charity, these three;
but the greatest of these [is] charity.*
-1 Corinthians 13:13

Day 5: Sow Seeds of Provision

But put ye on the Lord Jesus Christ, and make not provision for the flesh, to [fulfill] the lusts [thereof].

-Romans 13:14

Have you ever encountered a person who does not worry about the provision for tomorrow? People with this trait are not concerned with how God provides for daily physical needs; rather, they rest in the understanding that as they follow His vision and plan for their life, He faithfully supplies all their needs. Normally, this type of individual lives a very simple, yet strangely fulfilling, life. These kinds of people also gives freely to others. God can continue to pour into their life without having the concern of selfish lusts entering the picture, because they do not hold onto earthly treasure.

Elijah is a wonderful biblical example of making no fleshly provision (see 1 Kings 17:1-24). God sent Elijah to the brook Cherith. The word *Cherith* means "cutting", and thus indicates a season of pruning in Elijah's life when he had to rely completely on God. Elijah lived beside of the brook and was dependent on the ravens for the food they brought to him twice a day. Eventually, the brook dried up due to the drought. God already had plans for Elijah, though, once again, Elijah had to be willing to trust God for his provision.

The Father directed Elijah to Zarephath, where the Lord had prepared a widow to provide for him. Her situation was desperate. When Elijah met her, she was looking for wood to prepare a final meal for herself and her son. Elijah intersected her path and asked the unthinkable. He requested that she use her last provisions to prepare a meal for him. This widow's faith was expanded that day, for she gave all she had to Elijah. She sowed a seed of provision that could have cost not only her life, but her son's life as well. In return, God watered that seed and provided food until the drought was over for Elijah, the widow, and her son.

Sowing the Seeds

Pause for a moment to consider this truth concerning provision from God. For everyone who focuses on the Lord instead of on fleshly provisions, God provides for their needs in ways they could not provide for themselves. Allow God to show you where to sow your seeds of provision into the lives of others.

Seeds of Change Prayer

Lord, I want to be like the widow and be willing to give my all on behalf of another, as directed by You. Please give me discernment to hear Your voice, and allow me to not be led down a destructive path of enabling those who abuse a generous spirit of giving.

As I reflect upon sowing the seed of provision, I desire to find ways in my own life to live more like Elijah. Lead me to the brook of Cherith, the brook of "cutting", so that I may prosper in ways of faith. Let me also be sensitive to move upon Your first request and not wait for you to ask me again. By turning from the lust of the flesh and putting on the Lord Jesus Christ, I will live in a place of faith sustained by the Master's hand.

First Fruits

Record how God is instructing you to sow Seeds of Provision
and list what fruit it produces.

_____

_____

_____

_____

_____

_____

_____

_____

_____

_____

_____

_____

_____

_____

_____

_____

But put ye on the Lord Jesus Christ, and make not provision for the flesh,
to [fulfill] the lusts [thereof].
-Romans 13:14

Day 6: Sow Seeds of Temperance

But the fruit of the Spirit is love, joy, peace, longsuffering, gentleness, goodness, faith meekness, temperance: against such there is no law.

-Galatians 5:22-23

When we sow into a garden, we use many different types of seeds. They sprout, grow, and mature into something wholesome and delicious. When considering the topic of temperance (self-control), it is similar to a garden. As the seed of self-control matures, it affects many layers of our Christian walk in a healthy and wholesome way. When nurtured, self-control produces many types of fruit.

As we consider the definition of temperance, we understand that it is how we manage our desires and passions. Our ways are not His ways. Refinement of our life puts pressure upon us. We often release ourselves from this pressure by turning back to our own ways. We seek after our fleshly desires, not realizing what a beautiful vessel God wants to create with us. When we allow the loving Savior to tend to the needs of our heart, He begins to place inside of us new desires and passions.

A life of temperance is a healthy and beautiful balance of labor and rest. In order to be an effective witness for God, we must realize that even though we live in the world, we are not of the world. It is important to not chase after the things of the flesh, but rather seek after the Kingdom. The light of a life of self-control shines brightly in today's society of instant gratification. Not seeking the traditional desires and passions of the flesh allows us to sow memorable seeds of temperance into the lives of those we encounter.

Sowing the Seeds

One way to know that a believer is reaping the fruit of temperance is a life of balance between labor and rest. Examine your life. Is there balance? What are you pursuing? Lay aside your earthly pursuits and go after things of eternal significance.

Seeds of Change Prayer

I long for Your plan to replace the desires and passions I have for my life. Lord, I struggle with trying to define the path ahead instead of allowing You to have control. Today, Heavenly Father, please strengthen me where I am weak. Bring strength in my flesh, my mind, and my spirit, so I may be a light and sow seeds of temperance to those I meet along the way. Even if I am ridiculed for these lifestyle choices, help me to brush away any doubt and continue forward for Your glory.

First Fruits

Record how God is instructing you to sow Seeds of Temperance and list what fruit it produces.

_____

_____

_____

_____

_____

_____

_____

_____

_____

_____

_____

_____

_____

_____

_____

_____

But the fruit of the Spirit is love, joy, peace, longsuffering, gentleness, goodness, faith meekness, temperance: against such there is no law.
-Galatians 5:22-23

Day 7: Sow Seeds of Strength

God [is] our refuge and strength, a very present help in trouble.

-Psalms 46:1

We all face times of trouble or weakness in our life. Too many times, we stay on the frontlines and battle the difficulties alone. It is hard to understand why we do this. It might be for reasons of pride, a sense of accomplishment, or pure self-reliance. We lack faith to trust the One who gives strength. Instead of running to our refuge, we run to the problem. Instead of racing to the source of strength, we run to the point of weakness. All the while, God waits.

There comes a time that the battle is too large. Weary and worn, we collapse in exhaustion, handing over the reins to Him. God says, "Finally, I may come and fight for you!" He is there waiting all along, we simply must invite Him to help.

Our Father desires to sow daily seeds of strength into our life. Once planted in us, His seed of strength produces God-size results. Consider the accounts of Esther's mission to save the Jewish race, of Joshua with the collapse of the walls of Jericho, or of the beautiful story of Ruth. All were ordinary people who allowed God to sow strength into their lives.

Learning to run to God for refuge and strength is not always an easy task, especially for those with independent spirits. When we encounter people who are not yet relying fully on God's strength, we may see signs of discouragement. They may be at a place of utter loss of what to do next. With God's leading, it is up to us to sow into their lives the truths of how God is faithful to strengthen His children.

Sowing the Seeds

Encourage a friend today to lay down the battle that is overwhelming her life. Gently sow the seed of God's strength, and remind her that He is a very present help in her time of trouble.

Seeds of Change Prayer

Lord, I know my desire to be strong and independent does not mesh with Your desire for me to rely upon Your strength. So many times, I fall into the trap of exhaustion while fighting life's battles, only to be reminded to give the battle to You. Work in my life in such a way, that I will learn to run to my place of refuge at the first sign of struggle instead of a last resource to escape defeat. May my action of resting in Your strength draw others to You. As You sow strength into my life, may I be used to sow Your strength into the lives of others.

First Fruits

Record how God is instructing you to sow Seeds of Strength
and list what fruit it produces.

_____

_____

_____

_____

_____

_____

_____

_____

_____

_____

_____

_____

_____

_____

_____

_____

_____

_____

God [is] *our refuge and strength, a very present help in trouble.*
-Psalms 46:1

Day 8: Sow Seeds of Rest

And he said unto them, Come ye yourselves apart into a desert place, and rest a while: for there were many coming and going, and they had no leisure so much as to eat.

-Mark 6:31

From the very beginning, God provided an example of how we are to rest; nevertheless, it seems He must teach us this concept over and over again. God gives detailed instructions on how everything should take rest, even down to the land. Rest is so important that He instructs man to rest during both the plough and harvest times – two critical times in terms of agriculture. Heavy rains or lack thereof hinders the time to plough and spoils the time of reaping; yet, God specifically commanded a day of rest.

Jesus drew away on many occasions during His ministry on the earth. Most often, it was after an intense season of ministering to the needs of others. Why do you think God designed this specific model of rest? He intimately understands the demands of continual ministry.

For the disciples' sake, Jesus resolved the problem of rest by calling them away from the crowd. Notice that Jesus did not send the disciples away. Instead, He invited them to come away with Him. Jesus often led them to seek a quiet time in a place of isolation. They were fed both spiritually and physically in those moments alone with Him.

As we sow into the lives of others, we must remember to rest. For many of us, it is easy to recount endless days that we have been so busy, that we did not even take time to eat. Distractions of the world can easily fill even the time we intend to set aside for recharge. The enemy knows that if he can pull us away from rest and leisure time with Jesus, then we will become weak and worn. Rest is a critical building block needed for spiritual direction and vision.

Sowing the Seeds

Be aware that distractions are a weapon of the enemy. Guard your heart by finding time to be alone in His presence. Don't fall prey to believing you should only rest because you have nothing else to do, rather rest because of *all* you have to do. Recognize the value of resting in the presence of the One who gives you strength. Give up being busy for the sake of being busy and sow seeds of rest. You will emerge refreshed and ready to sow seeds in those around you.

Seeds of Change Prayer

Lord, forgive me for overlooking the power of resting in a desert place with You. Let me place a high priority on this time with You on a regular basis. Please lead me to opportunities of rest in solitude, especially after an exhausting season of labor or ministry. May I not continue down the path of self-destruction by overextending my time and energies, but rather look at Your model of how to stay refreshed physically, mentally, and spiritually. Your example of taking time away from the multitudes is a pattern for me to reflect upon, especially when I fall into temptation of laboring on behalf of others to the point of weariness.

First Fruits

Record how God is instructing you to sow Seeds of Rest
and list what fruit it produces.

_____

_____

_____

_____

_____

_____

_____

_____

_____

_____

_____

_____

_____

_____

_____

_____

_____

*And he said unto them, Come ye yourselves apart into a desert place, and rest a
while: for there were many coming and going,
and they had no leisure so much as to eat.*
-Mark 6:31

Part 2: Mental Seeds

Courage
Trust
Humility
Kindness
Honesty
Contentment
Respect
Stability

Tammy L Jordan

Day 9: Sow Seeds of Courage

*For God hath not given us the spirit of fear; but of
power, and of love, and of a sound mind.*
2 Timothy 1:7

Weeds of fear watered with worry can choke out the best
God-given purpose and plan. It is easy to fret over details. Faith
places us in an uncomfortable position of having to step into
God's path for our life, often without seeing how the next step
will unfold.

A review of the use of the word *courage* throughout the
Bible reveals interesting findings. When we decide to "be of
good courage", God can bring us to a different place, remove
fear, divide the difficulties, give direction, change our behavior,
cause us to put away obstacles and excuses, stir up power, and
remove dread. When we respond with the action that courage
brings to our lives, the Lord will move on our behalf and
strengthen us. Encouragement follows steps rooted in courage.
When we operate in courage, it produces a thankful heart
towards the way God delivers.

So as we proceed throughout the day, we should take a
measure of courage. The time invested in embracing it is well
spent. Courage deeply planted in our Lord's strength carries us
farther than we are able to imagine.

Sowing the Seeds

Think of a situation where you have responded in fear.
What would courage look like in that situation? Make a step to
act out of courage. Encourage yourself in the knowledge that
God's Word is true. He will deliver on His promise despite your
current circumstances.

Seeds of Change Prayer

Lord, remind me that fear and courage cannot reside in
the same step. May my path be grounded in Your strength.
Father, give me the power needed to take courage and release
fear. Please weed my life of things that stir up doubt, and

Father plant in me seeds of courage. Then I will grow in Your ways. Help this newly embraced courage reflect Your great power to those who need fear removed from their lives.

First Fruits

Record how God is instructing you to sow Seeds of Courage
and list what fruit it produces.

_____

_____

_____

_____

_____

_____

_____

_____

_____

_____

_____

_____

_____

_____

_____

_____

For God hath not given us the spirit of fear;
but of power, and of love, and of a sound mind.
-2 Timothy 1:7

Day 10: Sow Seeds of Trust

The God of my rock; in him will I trust: he is my shield, and the horn of my salvation, my high tower, and my refuge, my saviour; thou savest me from violence.

2 Samuel 22:3

It is easy to put our trust in many different things. Trust is placed in financial security, family relationships, a church, and even our ability to control the outcome of life. Things that are too big for us we often thrust into the 'trust God category'. We call upon Him to heal us, get us out of a financial stress, or repair a broken marriage. Trusting God with emergencies and eternity is one thing, but learning to trust Him with our day-to-day life seems to be much more difficult.

All throughout the Bible, we are reminded that God is our rock. He is our anchor when storms of life cause us to drift. Our Lord is a shield of protection from things both seen and unseen. The only requirement is that we surrender to His ways and follow Him close enough to enjoy the benefits of His protecting shield. When we learn to embrace Him as our shield, to nestle close to our Savior, He becomes our refuge in trying times as well as times of daily communion. When we trust Him to move and lead on our behalf, He has full power to deliver us from our oppressor. After reviewing the many times of personal delivery, why would we not daily place our trust in Him?

Sowing the Seeds

Do you have difficulty trusting God for the mundane? Think of an area in your life where you are depending on your own ability. Make a decision today to turn that situation over to God. Follow Him, fully believing that He will protect you as you journey. Sow seeds of trust and reap marvelous victory over the enemy.

Seeds of Change Prayer

Father, far too often, my refuge is my house, not You, Lord. Sadly, salvation in a difficult situation is found in personal abilities, not how You are able to keep me through any trial. The retreat that I seek is often vacation instead of restoration in Your high tower. Lord, how can I ever hope to claim You as my shield when I fail to place my trust fully in You. Please continue to teach me that Your ways are not my ways, and Your ways lead me to the Rock where I am to anchor every other aspect of my life. Let others notice the difference of how I behave in storms, so they too will come to trust in Your salvation.

Tammy L Jordan

First Fruits

Record how God is instructing you to sow Seeds of Trust
and list what fruit it produces.

_____

_____

_____

_____

_____

_____

_____

_____

_____

_____

_____

_____

_____

_____

_____

_____

_____

*The God of my rock; in him will I trust: he is my shield, and the horn of
my salvation, my high tower, and my refuge, my saviour;
thou savest me from violence.*
-2 Samuel 22:3

Day 11: Sow Seeds of Humility

...be clothed with humility: for God resisteth the proud, and giveth grace to the humble.

1 Peter 5:5

Humility is an important link in the ability to accept the gift of salvation. Each one of us must reach a place in life where we recognize that sin separates us from God. God resists the proud heart, because until that heart surrenders, He cannot work through it. The one who believes she is self-made, and that God has nothing to do with the rise and fall of her life is lost in pride. Only when this woman humbles herself, willingly admits that she is sinful, and accepts Jesus as the only way of salvation, will she receive the gift of Jesus' finished work on the cross.

Humility does not stop after we receive salvation. Many believers cling to a false humility. This personality artificially uses humility by belittling his or her abilities and talents in exchange for praise. This behavior elevates self-esteem for a fleeting moment. This elevated self-esteem soon needs another encounter to fill a void. Relying on others to build us up by pretending to lack something is an abuse of the precious seed of humility. God never intended for us to live in this fashion. He desires that we be clothed in *true* humility.

Transitioning from a lifestyle of false humility to a place of contentment takes time. We must begin by seeking after God's ways. He will bring us to a place in our life where we have a good and healthy grasp of what He has given us to use. It is important to know our limits. We must be able to release tasks to others as God directs. Laying claim to someone else's God-given field of labor will cause us to be ineffective and often result in a struggle with pride.

God uniquely shapes our gifts, talents, and abilities. We should not hide them away in a secret place, nor should we use them for self-glory. Rather, when we allow ourselves to be clothed in true humility, God can pour through the talents He has bestowed upon us. Our pride is set aside and does not get in the way or hinder our labors for Him.

Sowing the Seeds

True humility is a beautiful picture. Begin to develop your God-given talents. Do not negate the gifts and callings God has placed in your life. When someone recognizes a gifting in your life be thankful to God who created that gift in you. Being aware that all good gifts come from Him is the first step to sowing seeds of humility.

Seeds of Change Prayer

Lord, thank you for allowing me to come to a place of seeing myself through Your eyes. I praise you for allowing me to receive Your gift of salvation. Now Lord, please help me to seek Your ways, so I can be clothed in humility. Let pride be set aside in exchange for a surrendered life to You, and allow my unique calling to glorify You.

First Fruits

Record how God is instructing you to sow Seeds of Humility
and list what fruit it produces.

_____

_____

_____

_____

_____

_____

_____

_____

_____

_____

_____

_____

_____

_____

_____

_____

_____

_____

*...be clothed with humility: for God resisteth the proud,
and giveth grace to the humble.*
-1 Peter 5:5

Day 12: Sow Seeds of Kindness

She openeth her mouth with wisdom; and in her tongue is the law of kindness.

-Proverbs 31:26

Kindness is a trait easily overlooked in the world today. We should spend our lives speaking wisdom expressed in a manner of kindness. Responses of goodness and faithfulness should be customary. Seeds of kindness sown into the lives of others could influence this world in such a way that we could not measure its impact.

Kind behavior is to be our normal way of life. Even in difficult circumstances, we can speak the truth in a courteous manner. We should devote ourselves to allot the time needed to show acts of benevolence and service to those we love and strangers we meet. Far too often, seeds of kindness remain bound in the package of good intentions. Now is the time to remedy that problem.

Scattering kindness has the ability to remove hindrances in the lives of others. It uplifts the spirit in a way that few other acts can compare. When we allow our heart to follow the law of kindness, we leave our heart open to molding by the hands of our Father. Hardheartedness flees the soft pure light of unmerited favor.

Sowing the Seeds

Even in difficulty, we can be courteous. Common courtesy seems to be a lost art in today's society. Purpose in your heart to sow seeds of kindness into everyone you encounter. Some people will be skeptical; however, continue to be kind anyway. Sowing kindness does take time. Even with a hectic lifestyle, it is important to make it a priority in your life.

Seeds of Change Prayer

Lord, help me to control my tongue to such a degree that even in difficulties, I speak with kindness. May words of wisdom always be seasoned with mercy and grace. Let me be clothed in kindness so that others will be uplifted for Your kingdom.

First Fruits

Record how God is instructing you to sow Seeds of Kindness
and list what fruit it produces.

_____

_____

_____

_____

_____

_____

_____

_____

_____

_____

_____

_____

_____

_____

_____

_____

_____

_____

_____

_____

_____

She openeth her mouth with wisdom; and in her tongue is the law of kindness
-Proverbs 31:26

Day 13: Sow Seeds of Honesty

Pray for us: for we trust we have a good conscience, in all things willing to live honestly.

-Hebrews 13:18

So many times it is difficult to maintain a clear conscience; even more so, it is a challenge to live a life filled with honesty. Honesty is a seed that needs to be reproduced in great numbers in our society. We live in a world that expects God to ignore 'white lies' and to wink at dishonesty here and there in order to promote selfish gain in our life. Even as believers, temptation exists to rob us of the significant fruit of honesty, by sowing convenient half-truths instead of standing in full truth.

Hebrews 13:18, the intent was to have honesty in *all* things (not just some things). In this early age of Christianity, living honestly, standing for what they believed, and answering in truth cost many people their lives. As we reflect on what price has been paid over the centuries for answering in honesty and good conscience, we understand that these sacrifices have paved the way for Christianity to continue growing.

Sowing the seed of honesty into the life of others demands that we live honestly and speak God's truth in love. The Lord knows how important it is for us as believers to live honestly without the smallest hint of deceit. Being dishonest about small things in our life can really hinder others coming to know Him.

Sowing the Seeds

Take a moment to reflect on the condition of your heart today. Do you have a good conscience? Are you willing to live honestly in all things, even when it seems like you are sharing a harmless lies? Until you get to the place that you are willing to truly *live* an honest and wholesome life, you will remain crippled and unable to sow the important seed of honesty into the lives of those you encounter.

Seeds of Change Prayer

Father, remind me of the importance of maintaining my witness for You even when it is inconvenient. Help me to live my life honestly. As I sow Your words into the hearts of others, may I be able to sow them with a pure and genuine heart. Lord, purge my conscience of dishonesty, so that my words will match my true thoughts. Remind me that the fruit of honesty is sweet and satisfying to my soul. I know that dishonesty in my heart inhibits my effectiveness at reaching others for You. Surround me Lord with powerful prayer partners, so that I can always walk a path of honesty.

First Fruits

Record how God is instructing you to sow Seeds of Honesty
and list what fruit it produces.

_____

_____

_____

_____

_____

_____

_____

_____

_____

_____

_____

_____

_____

_____

_____

_____

Pray for us: for we trust we have a good conscience,
in all things willing to live honestly.
-Luke 8:15

Day 14: Sow Seeds of Contentment

[Let your] *conversation* [be] *without covetousness;*
[and be] *content with such things as ye have: for*
he hath said, I will never leave thee, nor forsake
thee.

-Hebrews 13:5

It is human nature to look around and become discontent with the path we walk in our Christian life. Contentment often evades us in times of trouble, especially when we get a glimpse into life of another that seems better than our own life. This behavior allows discouraging thoughts to take root in our mind.

There is a wonderful peace in knowing that Christ intimately knows our struggles. He faced difficulties and loss during His life on earth just as we do today. When we decide to be content and let contentment rule our life, it transitions us to a completely different level in our relationship with our Savior.

As a follower of Christ, we possess an unfailing strength because we walk in the strength of our Lord. We have immersed our life in the promise that He will never leave us or forsake us. The specific path we are walking does not matter, because God directs our journey.

We must ward off a negative attitude and stop wishing for our life to be like another's. It is important to lay hold of the life God has designed for us, a life that includes both mountains and valleys. The journey is what molds us into what He would have us to be. If we just picked the highlights in life, we would never learn how to endure. Our faith would fail to grow, and it would always take something bigger and better to keep us satisfied.

It is important not to confuse contentment with complacency. We are to accept where God has placed us, yet continue to press forward. Our task is to persist in making progress in our Christian walk. We are to stay focused on the Savior and not on the condition or circumstances of life. He will lead us through the seasons of difficulties if we continually walk with Him. Making a commitment to walking in His strength will allow us to scatter seeds of contentment to those we meet.

Sowing the Seeds

Finding a balance between contentment and complacency is not easy. Begin by focusing on what you have instead of what you lack. Be grateful to God for the measure He has poured into you. Sow the seeds He has given you and wait for the harvest. As you begin the season of harvest, look for new soil and new seeds as you move forward to the calling God has for your life.

Seeds of Change Prayer

Lord, I know that my eyes wander at times, and I don't often understand why my path seems more difficult than those around me. God, please help me adjust my vision to see Your work in my life. I desire to claim Your unfailing strength and apply that strength where I am weak. When I feel alone and abandoned, let me not fall into the trap of discouragement; rather, allow me to rest in the promise that You are forever walking beside of me as I follow Your leading.

First Fruits

Record how God is instructing you to sow Seeds of Contentment
and list what fruit it produces.

_____

_____

_____

_____

_____

_____

_____

_____

_____

_____

_____

_____

_____

_____

_____

_____

*[Let your] conversation [be] without covetousness; [and be] content with
such things as ye have: for he hath said,
I will never leave thee, nor forsake thee.*
-Hebrews 13:5

Day 15: Sow Seeds of Respect

*Though the Lord be high, yet hath he respect unto
the lowly: but the proud he knoweth afar off.*
                                        -Psalms 138:6

How many times have we found ourselves giving due respect to those in authority? Often, we show respect to our parents, our pastor, a favorite teacher, or a mentor. Other times we hold respect in our hearts for a position that a person holds such as a firefighter or a famous athlete. Seeds of respect are easily justified and deserved in these situations.

Do we ever think about whom God respects? We understand that earthly fathers hold respect for their children. Therefore, since God is our Heavenly Father, it is easy to see how the Lord holds His children in high regard.

God's view of His children is very different from a worldly view of respect. The world uplifts and gives attention to popular musicians, sport stars, and actors. Worldly popularity fails to factor in lifestyle choices or personal conduct. However, God views the heart. God is far above us, yet His respect belongs to those who learn to be humble servants. He esteems the servant and holds them in a place of respect. In sharp contrast, the proud, those with an arrogant attitude, are in a distant place away from Him.

Sowing the Seeds

Where do you sow seeds of respect? Are you tempted to sow into popular opinion, or do you reserve your seeds of respect for the humble individual, often a person never noticed in a crowd? It is time to consider how God shows respect. Allow Him to distant your heart from the proud and turn your attention and admiration to the overlooked, lowly believer.

Seeds of Change Prayer

Father, change the way I sow seeds of respect. May I uplift the ones who are humble and sold out to You and shy away from those who are self-elevated. Give me words of encouragement that I may shower Your servants with the knowledge that You are observing their labors with great respect. Lord, teach me to seek a life of humility and not one of glory, so that my daily walk will be one that is distinguished in Your eyes.

First Fruits

Record how God is instructing you to sow Seeds of Respect
and list what fruit it produces.

_____

_____

_____

_____

_____

_____

_____

_____

_____

_____

_____

_____

_____

_____

_____

*Though the Lord be high, yet hath he respect unto the lowly:
but the proud he knoweth afar off.*
-Psalms 138:6

Day 16: Sow Seeds of Stability

And wisdom and knowledge shall be the stability of thy times, and strength of salvation: the fear of the LORD is his treasure.

-Isaiah 33:6

Most of us have faced moments when our world shakes to its very foundation. There are many normal reactions to this type of situation. Some reactions include fear, resentment, anger, exhaustion, and helplessness. How we respond in this time of extreme crisis will often determine the course of our life for years to come. If we succumb to the temptation of letting anger turn to bitterness, we will lose joy. Collapsing into self-pity prevents us from moving forward with God. Fear can paralyze any valid future decisions, and unresolved exhaustion will deter progress. When this period of crisis occurs, we find stability removed from our today and for an unknown amount of time in the future. With the daily framework of our life destroyed, we begin seeking how to regain a steady positive flow to everyday life.

We should find our solution by diving into the scripture in search of stability for difficult times. We are not able to escape valley experiences, but God has given us the resources of wisdom and knowledge to guide us through the rebuilding process. He will return us to a stable place in Him, even though the situation we face may not change.

Wisdom and knowledge combine to give us discernment, perception, and the skill to step forward with God's leading. In wisdom, we allow Him to direct and are able to follow His guidance. Faith is the framework built upon the foundation of salvation in Him. It will provide security in any situation. It is faith that allows us to weather the fiercest storm in a place of peace. The more we face, the more we expand our understanding of how the Lord calms our heart and brings solid ground on which to stand in any circumstance. Placing trust in Him adds strength to encourage us to rest in His salvation. So whatever state we find our lives, we must place all of our treasures in the hands of our Father. With that action, He will add immeasurable stability to any situation.

Sowing the Seeds

Find a scripture for your circumstance. Stand on that scripture no matter what the situation looks like. Declare His Word over your life. Do not waiver. He is your strong tower, and His promises are true and faithful.

Seeds of Change Prayer

Oh Father, I desire Your strength and stability in a world that quickly changes. My past proved to me that You are my only true source of stability. Please pour into me Your wisdom to review life circumstances from a Heavenly perspective. Help me to turn over any crisis to You, so that You are able to guide me forward and, in turn, help me to sow seeds of stability in others.

Tammy L Jordan

Record how God is instructing you to sow Seeds of Stability
and list what fruit it produces.

_____

_____

_____

_____

_____

_____

_____

_____

_____

_____

_____

_____

_____

_____

_____

*And wisdom and knowledge shall be the stability of thy times,
and strength of salvation: the fear of the LORD is his treasure.*
-Isaiah 33:6

54

Part 3: Emotional Seeds

Encouragement
Truth
Honor
Gratitude
Unity
Goodness
Boldness
Integrity

Tammy L Jordan

Day 17: Sow Seeds of Encouragement

Behold, God [is] mine helper: the Lord [is] with them that uphold my soul.

-Psalms 54:4

We have all encountered a time that we needed external input to get through the day. In a time of emptiness, we reach out for our support system. Seeds of encouragement are to the heart what a trellis is to a plant.

When we think back to a time when we received much-needed intervention, we often remember the emotions. Usually,, the help received during those times did not solve the problem. Rather the seed of encouragement simply sustained us for the moment. It provided time to catch our breath and gave us the support needed to return to the challenge. Encouragement may come in the form of a simple act of kindness, a physical deed of help, or a few short words that allow us to endure a difficult leg of the journey.

As the sower, we may never know what a seed of encouragement does for another. It may be the breath of fresh air needed to turn their life in a different direction. Sowing encouragement is a unique experience. Encouragement promotes understanding that binds two hearts together for one purpose. When we encourage another, we lay aside thoughts of self, and pour into the life of one that needs uplifting. Being a vessel used to encourage is quite fascinating. The Lord appears on the scene and is with the encourager. If we desire to have the Lord by our side, maybe we should open the door to Him by encouraging another person whose soul needs refreshed.

Sowing the Seeds

Encouragement is not always easy. It is difficult to look at someone going through trying circumstances and find a way to encourage them. It can be especially difficult if their situation reminds you of a trial you have faced in your own life. Be careful not to let their troubles overwhelm you. *Instead*, find strength in the Lord and encourage them to find Him in the midst of their storm. You may be surprised to find that your greatest personal encouragement comes when you are encouraging others.

Seeds of Change Prayer

Lord, make me aware of the needs of those around me. Please give me words or actions to uphold others during a difficult moment. I know that You are with me and directing my steps to sow appropriate seeds of encouragement. Soften my heart to bend to Your leading.

Record how God is instructing you to sow Seeds of
Encouragement
and list what fruit it produces.

_____

_____

_____

_____

_____

_____

_____

_____

_____

_____

_____

_____

_____

_____

_____

Behold God [is] mine helper:
the Lord [is] with them that uphold my soul.
-Psalms 54:4

Day 18: Sow Seeds of Truth

> *That we* [henceforth] *be no more children, tossed to and fro, and carried about with every wind of doctrine... But speaking the truth in love, may grow up into him in all things...*
> -Ephesians 4:14-15

Truth is a powerful seed to sow. So powerful, we are given specific instructions on how to sow it. The seed of truth carries great impact and it has a clearly defined planting time. This time is revealed to us as God opens the door, and He goes before the seed bearer opening up the ground of another's heart.

Sometimes sharing truth does not always go as planned. In Galatians 4:16 Paul writes, "Am I therefore become your enemy, because I tell you the truth?" Yet further reading in Galatians reveals that Paul was not discouraged. He pressed forward and wrote one of the most well-known passages in the Bible, The Fruits of the Spirit. This portion of scripture speaks of the results of Christ dwelling in the believer. The Holy Spirit in us promotes growth and development as a believer. When we grow as a Christian, we are no longer carried about by the wind of untrue doctrine, but begin to share His truth to those around us wrapped in love. As we sow truth of things pertaining to the Spirit, the harvest is everlasting life to those who open their hearts to His truth.

Seeds of truth are not just sown into the lives of unbelievers, but may also need to be sown into the hearts of fellow believers. Especially for young believers, sometimes it is difficult to initially comprehend deeper truths. Again, this is a delicate seed sowing process. God will position us as He leads to share His truth, particularly concerning untrue doctrine that leads people away from foundational truths. The Father willingly sends mature Christians, firmly rooted in His Word, to help new believers develop into mature disciples. This growth not only strengthens the new believer, but also the entire body of Christ.

The hardest seeds of truth to be sown may be those for mature believers. Even the wisest Christian can become distracted and led away from the truth, much like Peter. God will send a very strong disciple to speak truth into them. In Peter's case, God used Paul (see Galatians). This type of seed is most often sown face-to-face, is deeply planted, and can at times initially be rejected. It is important as a believer, regardless of our maturity in Christ, to remain open to His truth sown into our lives. In time, believers usually surrender to God's seed of truth sown in love by a fellow believer.

Sowing the Seeds

Truth is very important. However, it is important to note that just because something is the truth doesn't mean it has to be said. Furthermore, it doesn't mean it has to be said by you.

It is very important to learn to follow the leading of the Spirit when it comes to sowing truth in others. Truth sown before it's time will destroy instead of heal. If you sow truth that isn't yours to sow, the receiver may reject it. Be sensitive not only to what God wants you to sow, but to the timing as well.

Seeds of Change Prayer

Father, as I sow seeds of truth, prepare my heart to bear such a precious role in another's life. Spewing the truth in a fit of anger or condemnation will not yield the desired growth. Help me wrap up truth in words of love. I pray for it to not just be ordinary love, but a vulnerable love that comes from deep within the soul. I desire to share in a love that is reflective of Your love for me. It is in this time as the seed sower, I must allow You to prepare me as much as the person receiving the message of truth.

First Fruits

Record how God is instructing you to sow Seeds of Truth
and list what fruit it produces.

_____

_____

_____

_____

_____

_____

_____

_____

_____

_____

_____

_____

_____

_____

_____

_____

*That we [henceforth] be no more children, tossed to and fro,
and carried about with every wind of doctrine... But speaking
the truth in love, may grow up into him in all things...*
-Ephesians 4:14-15

Day 19: Sow Seeds of Honor

Honour the LORD with thy substance, and with the firstfruits of all thine increase.

-Proverbs 3:9

We can only sow the seed we have. If we lack a certain seed, then we have to obtain that seed in order to sow it. Honor is a seed that is becoming rare in the world around us. Honoring parents seems old-fashioned, as is honoring our Lord.

According to Proverbs 15:33: "The fear of the LORD is the instruction of wisdom, and before honour is humility." Therefore, we must be willing to sow into the ways of humility, before we can reap honor. It is easy to see why honor is being eroded from everyday life.

Not everyone wants to live a life in submission to our Savior. It is difficult to remove self from the equation, weaken our pride, and acknowledge that we are not able to save ourselves. We must rely upon God to deliver us. This level of reliance brings us to a place of humility. There we find the seeds of honor.

Living honorably means being willing to follow the way of righteousness and embracing things that are ethical. In addition, we need to be willing to show mercy and deep compassion, just as God showed mercy to us.

As we learn to walk a walk worthy of obtaining honor, we make a commitment to refrain from returning to former self-reliant paths. Pride will destroy or bring down a life, but honor will lift up one that is humble. We do not need to seek after ways to elevate ourselves. God will shine through a humble spirit and lift us up. He desires our light to shine for Him.

Sowing the Seeds

Humble your heart. Seek after righteousness and mercy. God is faithful to bestow honor unto our lives. When honor is present, you willingly give of your first fruits, your increase, your substance, and your very life in order for Him to use you for His glory. Simply desire to honor God and then you will have seeds of honor to sow.

Seeds of Change Prayer

Lord Jesus, I long to give honor to Your name in both word and action. Mold my life as a potter molds the clay into a vessel of honor. May I be willing to humble my life before You, seek after Your ways of truth and righteousness, and never fail to show mercy even unto those who wish to do harm. Help me to live in a respectable way so I am able to sow seeds of honor into the lives of others.

First Fruits

Record how God is instructing you to sow Seeds of Honor
and list what fruit it produces.

_____

_____

_____

_____

_____

_____

_____

_____

_____

_____

_____

_____

_____

_____

_____

_____

Honour the LORD with thy substance, and with the
firstfruits of all thine increase.
-Proverbs 3:9

Day 20: Sow Seeds of Gratitude

*As ye have therefore received Christ Jesus the
Lord, so walk ye in him; Rooted and built up in
him, and stablished in the faith, as ye have been
taught, abounding therein with thanksgiving.*
-Colossians 2:6-7

We have so much to be grateful for in life. Even when
things are not perfect and storms are raging, as a believer, we
have our Rock to cling to in times of trouble. It is easy to get
caught up in being thankful for the big things in life, things like
a new house, a big promotion, or the birth of a child. However,
when we seek to have a grateful spirit in the small things in life,
we abide in a place of rejoicing.

As our faith deepens in the rich soil of God's salvation,
we lay hold of the concept that our spirit should daily overflow
with thanksgiving. This one change in our attitude allows us to
sow seeds of gratitude to those we encounter on our journey.
When we walk in the ways of Christ, we begin to see that each
day is a gift and an opportunity to share His love with those
around us.

Becoming rooted in His ways takes a willing spirit. We
must embrace opportunities to grow in our faith. This growth
may place us in a position that feels uncomfortable. However,
our Father is faithful to walk beside of us and even to send
others to comfort and uplift our hearts. Through this
experience, we learn to be grateful for the smallest provisions.
Others notice this growth, and a truly thankful heart sows
seeds of God's power to change lives forever.

Sowing the Seeds

Take time every day to be grateful. Focus on the small
things. What things have you taken for granted? Where do
you see God's provision like never before? Thank God for all He
is doing in your life, and be willing to share this gratitude with
others.

Seeds of Change Prayer

Lord, help me to see Your greater plan for my life. Let me be thankful for the big things and grateful for the little ways that You decide to use me. May my eyes be opened to the reality that we have such a short time on earth to share Your salvation with those around us. Help me to maintain a grateful approach to simple things in life as well as difficult storms so that others are drawn to You.

First Fruits

Record how God is instructing you to sow Seeds of Gratitude
and list what fruit it produces.

_____

_____

_____

_____

_____

_____

_____

_____

_____

_____

_____

_____

_____

_____

_____

_____

*As ye have therefore received Christ Jesus the Lord, so walk ye in
him; Rooted and built up in him, and stablished in the faith, as
ye have been taught, abounding therein with thanksgiving.*
-Colossians 2:6-7

Day 21: Sow Seeds of Unity

Behold, how good and how pleasant [it is] for brethren to dwell together in unity!

-Psalms 133:1

Dwelling together in unity in marriage, extended family relationships, and as the body of Christ is an important step of growth that leads to maturity. Unity takes self-control, cooperation, negotiation, and refinement of our prideful nature. When we do not agree with another person, it does not mean we cannot work together for the greater good. No two people will agree on every decision.

Often we wish to confuse unity with uniformity. Unity is all different pieces working together. Uniformity is all pieces being the same. God created us as unique individuals. He equips us with different personalities and talents for His glory. If we were all just alike, we would be able to accomplish little as the body of Christ. Our sameness would cripple us as a unit. A well-developed team has one purpose in mind, but that team comprises more than one type of personality. Diversity in a group striving together with one purpose will bring strength.

Unity is such a precious seed. It can heal marriages, restore families, and be one of the single biggest factors to church growth and successful ministries. The next time we are faced with differences that can lead to defeat, take time to explore how two, united for the same cause, are stronger than two acting as individuals. Unity may stretch us to find a third way of doing something, and that growth in maturity will propel the entire task forward more quickly and with greater results. Unity will never ask us to surrender our core beliefs as a Christian. Rather, God will bring other like-minded believers to work in the same vineyard. However, we must be willing to lay down our preconceived ideas of how things need to be accomplished in exchange for His greater plan to move forward. Then we will see firsthand how good and pleasant it is to dwell in unity as believers.

Sowing the Seeds

By embracing the concept that unity is not the same as uniformity we can get beyond our way of doing things and seek fully after God's way of accomplishing a task with the help of others. So often, we are too busy trying to mold fellow believers into our image that we forget that our goal should be all believers formed in His image. Accept the differences, and find something positive about every person you meet. Consider what they have to bring to the team.

Seeds of Change Prayer

Lord, help me to lay aside my ideas and ownership of a project to embrace fellow laborers that You have assembled for a similar purpose. May I never let differences within the team dictate the accomplishment of the group. I desire to let You lead me to a greater maturity as a believer, so I may be used to unite rather than tear apart a ministry or personal relationships.

First Fruits

Record how God is instructing you to sow Seeds of Unity
and list what fruit it produces.

_____

_____

_____

_____

_____

_____

_____

_____

_____

_____

_____

_____

_____

_____

_____

Behold, how good and how pleasant [it is] *for brethren
to dwell together in unity!*
-Psalms 133:1

Day 22: Sow Seeds of Goodness

I had fainted unless I had believed to see the goodness of the Lord in the land of the living.
-Psalms 27:13

In a world where difficulties abound, it is easy to get buried in the mud of life. People forsake us, lives are tossed about, and a state of distress becomes our normal way of life. Weariness often sets in during life's storms. So often, we just go through the motions of life instead of dwelling in the land of the living, which requires us to first grow in faith.

Dwelling in the land of the living, means living in the moment of today and leaving the past behind. When we carry the burdens of yesterday, the reality of today, and the worry of tomorrow, we inhibit our ability to function properly. It is easy to become overwhelmed to the point of giving up and almost fainting from the combined weights. God never intended life to be this complicated. That is why so often in scripture He compels us to bring our burdens to Him and leave them in His capable hands. Living in today allows us to rest in knowing that God holds tomorrow and that the past continues to work together for good for His children.

In this growth period, we see the goodness of God. Pause for a moment to consider His vast and immeasurable works. No past, present, or future event in our life is beyond His ability to mold, transform, and refine for good. His goodness protects, strengthens, and renews our weary spirits. When we start seeking for His labors in our life, a renewing of energy takes place. We begin to live again! It is time to dust off the past, embrace the present, and follow Him for our future. We must seek Him while He may be found in the land of the living. He is waiting to revive a fainting heart. Once our hearts are uplifted, we can plant a seed in the life of others, so they too may see the goodness of our Lord.

Sowing the Seeds

When we carry the burdens of yesterday, the reality of today, and the worry of tomorrow, we inhibit our ability to function properly. Lay aside the burdens of what happened yesterday. Realize that God's mercies are new every morning. Find ways to enjoy today. While it is important to plan for tomorrow, it is also important that you don't get so caught up in tomorrow that you miss today. Partake in the goodness that comes only from Him.

Seeds of Change Prayer

Father, comfort me in difficult times so that I do not become so focused on the problems that I forget to live. Let me instead observe Your goodness, even through the storms. Remove from me a negative spirit so that others may see how You daily sow goodness into the lives of Your children.

First Fruits

Record how God is instructing you to sow Seeds of Goodness
and list what fruit it produces.

_____

_____

_____

_____

_____

_____

_____

_____

_____

_____

_____

_____

_____

_____

_____

_____

*I had fainted unless I had believed to see the goodness of the
Lord in the land of the living.*
-Psalms 27:13

Day 23: Sow Seeds of Boldness

Let us therefore come boldly unto the throne of grace, that we may obtain mercy, and find grace to help in time of need.

-Hebrews 4:16

How often does fear prevent us following God's plans? Sometimes even small requests to step out by faith cause us to stop dead in our tracks, and other times there are huge leaps of faith where we sit back and wait. We lack confidence in God's timing and direction. Sadly, even after an instance of lagging faith, we may question why God is not using us in a big way. Today, we will look at the simple answer. We lack a key ingredient in Christian development and that ingredient is boldness.

There are several stages of boldness. In the beginning, we stand openly before a righteous God. The Holy Spirit has drawn us, and we expose our sins in order to have those sins covered by the blood of Christ. This exchange allows us to stand boldly before the throne of grace where we obtain mercy. His grace is a gift far beyond what we deserve. It fills us with a new boldness, a confidence in our Heavenly Father that will carry us for a season in life when we will learn to lean upon Him for help in our time of need.

However, we all reach a point where God desires to help with the maturing process and He presents a choice in our path. To follow the path that He presents requires a boldness of spirit. The only thing that stands in the way is the fear of the unknown. Once we embrace the path that He places before us, He will steadily increase our ability to be His hands and feet. During this phase of boldness training, we learn to see the Lord working on our behalf. We look for Him and His leading. When God speaks into our lives, we listen, and we can proclaim boldly the power of the cross. This new growth allows us to be used in a powerful way.

There is one final way to completely embrace the boldness in Christ. Hebrews 13:6 says "...we may boldly say, The Lord is my helper, and I will not fear what man shall do unto me." When we fully understand that the Lord is all we need (He is our strength and help), we will lay down fear that paralyzes our Christian service. We will boldly sow seeds of the story of the cross. Wherever He leads us, we will follow, because we do not fear what man can do to us. As we follow Him, we experience the joy of what God can do through us.

Sowing the Seeds

Think of a current choice in your life that is requiring you to sow seeds of boldness. What is holding you back? Step out in faith and follow what God has for your life. As the Lord begins to move in your situation then declare His power in your life. Set aside the fear of what man wants and follow what God wants for your life.

Seeds of Change Prayer

Thank You God for Your gift of mercy. Thank you for covering my sins with the blood of Jesus. Help me to grow in boldness. Take away fear and allow me to follow You. Use me to proclaim the power of the cross. God help me not to seek to please man, but rather to please You. Lord, be my strength as I do Your work and joyfully sow seeds of boldness into the lives of others.

Record how God is instructing you to sow Seeds of Boldness
and list what fruit it produces.

_____

_____

_____

_____

_____

_____

_____

_____

_____

_____

_____

_____

_____

_____

_____

_____

*Let us therefore come boldly unto the throne of grace, that we
may obtain mercy, and find grace to help in time of need.*
-Hebrews 4:16

Day 24: Sow Seeds of Integrity

The just man walketh in his integrity: his children are blessed after him.

-Proverbs 20:7

There are times in life we have an opportunity to do what is honorable, even when no other soul is there to see the choice we make. We may even bear the costs associated with the right path. It is in that quiet hidden moment of seeking the honorable path verses the easy way that we understand what it means to walk in integrity. There may not be a pat on the back or a proclamation of a job well done because righteousness was chosen over wrong. The outcome of sowing seeds of integrity is far greater than a mere nod of approval from peers. Morally based decisions made today mean that we believe in a future harvest tomorrow. The future harvest is a harvest that our children will reap.

Often we spend our lives seeking ways to build up security for our families, to protect them from harm, to preserve them when we are no longer part of their daily lives. It is common to have insurance in place for major life events, trust funds prepared, and nest eggs tucked away for a time we wish to bless children. While it is wise to make provisions for future generations, the best way we can secure blessings for those following us is to be righteous in character, which prompts us to sow seeds of integrity.

Integrity is a seed that reaps blessings. Once salvation is accepted, we should desire to study with intensity the ways of Christ so we may walk within His footsteps. When we become true followers of His lifestyle, our lives are made whole, our spirits are undivided, and we are clothed in His righteousness. It is easy to understand how honorable choices preserve our testimony and integrity. Future blessings for our children depend upon our actions today. Sow integrity and allow our children to reap the blessings.

Sowing the Seeds

Morally based decisions made today mean you believe in a future harvest. The next time you find yourself faced with a hard decision, consider the consequences for the future generations. Are you sowing seeds of integrity or seeds of destruction to your children? Make a choice to do the right thing. Leave a spiritual legacy for your future descendants.

Seeds of Change Prayer

Jesus, give me the strength I need to choose the right path, even when it is difficult. When I falter and desire to seek the easy path, remind me that a life sowing into the ways of integrity creates an environment where children are blessed.

First Fruits

Record how God is instructing you to sow Seeds of Integrity
and list what fruit it produces.

_____

_____

_____

_____

_____

_____

_____

_____

_____

_____

_____

_____

_____

_____

_____

The just man walketh in his integrity:
his children are blessed after him.
-Proverbs 20:7

Part 4: Spiritual Seeds

Mercy
Meekness
Peace
Grace
Longsuffering
Virtue
Faith
Patience

Tammy L Jordan

Day 25: Sow Seeds of Mercy

*Mercy and truth are met together; righteousness
and peace have kissed [each other].*

-Psalms 85:10

The beautiful passage of Psalms 85:7-13 reveals to us a glimpse of what mercy does in the life of a believer. When we come to the Father through Jesus, He must show us great mercy. We do not deserve the favor that He bestows upon us. In fact, we deserve quite the opposite. He grants us the gift of salvation – this cherished seed of mercy – because He understands that mercy planted in our hearts opens up the opportunity to have a relationship with Him. Salvation develops a foundation on which the Father can build and speak words of peace and comfort into our hearts.

God never intended for truth to be shared without mercy because truth without mercy extracts peace from our life. The truth is that we are separated from God by sin, and the payment is something we cannot make on our own. Then God's mercy met the truth of our sin debt on the cross. There, at this agonizing place of torture and pain, mercy was poured out and paid the price for all mankind. It was in this moment, the righteousness of God can now kiss the face of humanity through Christ's sacrifice.

Mercy allows God's truth to spring forth from believers here on earth. It gives hope to a world searching for peace. Our Father gives good gifts to His children. He promises to walk before us in the way He would have us to go. We must willingly let His truth flow through us, but always be willing to season it with mercy. As God was merciful to us, we too must be willing to sow seeds of mercy to those whom we encounter. When mercy and truth combine, the righteousness of God's mercy and the peace found in truth will kiss in a sweet embrace.

Sowing the Seeds

It has been said that the truth hurts. However, many times the reason truth inflicts pain is that the truth is shared without the seasoning of mercy. Practice combining truth with large amounts of mercy. When a person knows you care about them, they are more willing to listen to the truth you share. Be aware of the mercy you have received and be willing to pass that mercy on to others. Remember often, that you received the gift of salvation while you were yet in a wretched state of sin and despair. Your fellow believer is no less deserving of mercy than you were at the point God intervened. Thank God for His mercy.

Seeds of Change Prayer

Lord Jesus, I praise you for Your mercy. I'm grateful that Your salvation is near me. Thank You for teaching me to walk in Your way. Direct my steps so that I too may share Your truth with others and sow seeds of mercy, so others experience Your peace in their life.

First Fruits

Record how God is instructing you to sow Seeds of Mercy
and list what fruit it produces.

_____

_____

_____

_____

_____

_____

_____

_____

_____

_____

_____

_____

_____

_____

_____

*Mercy and truth are met together; righteousness
and peace have kissed* [each other].
-Psalms 85:10

Day 26: Sow Seeds of Meekness

...the meek shall inherit the earth; and shall delight themselves in the abundance of peace.
-Psalms 37:11

Meekness is often viewed as an undesirable trait. Learning to walk in meekness, including learning to properly turn the other cheek, takes much self-discipline. Sometimes living a life of meekness means walking away from an argument that has escalated into inappropriate name calling, even though we may be winning the fight. Instead of slandering another, we silently remove ourselves from the conversation. It takes discernment to know when to stand and battle, and when it is appropriate to allow another the last word. Great effort is required to restrain our words, especially when we are right.

In the struggle to walk in meekness, it is helpful to turn to a powerful example of what it means to walk this path. Christ is a pure example of living a meek life. His life was not boastful, but meekness did not cause Him to act as a doormat. Reading about the life of Christ, we see many examples where He stood and reproved others. Later on, He sustained unimaginable injury for our sake. He took the weight of our sin on the cross, rather than return judgment to all of humanity.

We must reach a point where, weak by the world's standards, we bear whatever cross we are called to bear in life. In this calm, diminished role, His strength can be revealed. Meekness is a powerful seed that returns great harvests to the sower of this seed.

When we consider the harvest produced by living a meek life, we encounter a very special promise. Upon the Lord's return, the meek, will inherit the earth while those who do not believe in the Lord will be separated from God. However, we do not have to wait for eternity to enjoy the harvest of this seed. During this life here on earth, meek servants of Christ, can take possession of new territory for our Lord. This new territory is in the form of winning the souls of others to Him. When Christ adorns us with the beauty of His sacrifice, His glory will shine in our life and draw others to the finished work on the cross. Sowing seeds of meekness is worth the discipline needed to control our impulse response to others. We must let Jesus be the example of how we should reply to those who seek to degrade us.

Sowing the Seeds

Study Christ's example of a life of meekness. Learn how He handles conflict. Notice that He did not let anyone run over Him or change His point of view on the truth. However, nowhere in scripture do we find Christ lashing out in uncontrollable anger at those who sought to destroy Him. Even though He boldly reproved individuals and groups of people, Jesus remained true to His calling and delivered truth without sin. Let Jesus be your example as you seek to live a life filled with seeds of meekness.

Seeds of Change Prayer

Lord, teach me to control my initial response to others that would unnecessarily inflict injury or pain into their life. Let my response reflect Your ways. Give me strength to be bold when boldness is required, and obedience to walk away silently when silence is needed. May I not look at a meek spirit as undesirable, but rather as the very essence of how You describe Yourself. Give me a desire to learn of Your ways, so that I too am able to find rest for my soul.

First Fruits

Record how God is instructing you to sow Seeds of Meekness
and list what fruit it produces.

_____

_____

_____

_____

_____

_____

_____

_____

_____

_____

_____

_____

_____

_____

_____

_____

...the meek shall inherit the earth; and shall delight themselves in
the abundance of peace.
-Psalms 37:11

Day 27: Sow Seeds of Peace

Peace I leave with you, my peace I give unto you:
not as the world giveth, give I unto you. Let not
your heart be troubled, neither let it be afraid.

-John 14:27

We live in a society where peace does not abound. In fact, our world is quite the opposite of a peaceful place. We hear news of distress, wars, and fighting each day. Exposure to disagreements and fighting even in familial relationships can lead us to seek after a sanctuary of peace. Many times, we turn to artificial peace or peace that is fleeting. In difficult times, we may seek new relationships to replace ones that are disintegrating, entrap ourselves with excessive work to limit quiet time, or embrace an addiction that allows us to temporarily check out of life. We seek peace in vacations that end, financial stability that may crumble overnight, fleshly relationships that fade away, and injurious habits that leave us empty over time. This fleeting peace leaves us more depleted than before we sought after it. Our Savior desires to fill us with a different kind of peace–*His Peace.*

God sent His only Son to a world that was without hope to bring a peace that supersedes all other forms of worldly peace. When we are willing to embrace wisdom, which is God's plan of salvation, we find happiness and paths of peace. This does not mean that conflict is removed every step of the way. Rather, we now have a Savior that sows an everlasting seed of peace into our life. We understand according to Psalms 37:37, the end of the upright man's life is peace. This is God's faithful promise to His children. Even though peace may not initially be present during difficult events that come into our life, we do have the assurance of eternal peace for the believer. While the thought of our future home in Heaven sustains us, sometimes we desperately need God to work in our life today.

When we live a life that is spiritually minded, He can bring us to a state of peace in the midst of chaos. The Father can deliver the unthinkable into the life of a Christian. It is encouraging to reflect upon the times God has intervened on our behalf to deflate hostility towards us from an enemy. He walks before us as a shield and extends to us a path of peace even in the presence of our enemies. This is when the Lord can fight for us. Sadly, we normally do not wait upon Him. We negate our own peace and prohibit Him from building a bridge to our enemies. It further destroys that opportunity for the Father to use us to present the gospel of peace.

When we take time to embrace the wisdom of Christ and fully surrender our ways to His ways of peace, then He can do great and mighty things to deliver us from distress. To harvest the fruit of righteousness (salvation), it must first be sown into the lives of others by the hands of those who walk in the way of Godly peace. As believers, we are to sow this seed into a world that is desperate for peace. It is important to scatter the seeds of a heavenly peace to all we encounter on our journey.

Sowing the Seeds

Make your home a place of peace. Don't count on fleeting times, like vacation, for your rest. Find your rest in the peace that comes from knowing God is in control of your life. When you are under attack, wait for God to intervene in your behalf. Rest assured that the enemy cannot harm you when you are following after the Lord. Be careful not to jump into action ahead of His protection. Allow Him to lead you and you will find His perfect peace.

Seeds of Change Prayer

Father, help me to rest my life in Your hands so I may claim Your peace that passes understanding. Remind me that You have given me a different kind of peace. I find a greater sense of Your peace working in my life as I submit to Your wisdom. Help me be patient as You work out the details to bring about peaceful results, even when I'm dealing with difficult situations.

First Fruits

Record how God is instructing you to sow Seeds of Peace
and list what fruit it produces.

_____

_____

_____

_____

_____

_____

_____

_____

_____

_____

_____

_____

_____

_____

_____

_____

Peace I leave with you, my peace I give unto you:
not as the world giveth, give I unto you.
Let not your heart be troubled, neither let it be afraid.
-John 14:27

Day 28: Sow Seeds of Grace

For by grace are ye saved through faith; and that not of yourselves: it is the gift of God: Not of works, lest any man should boast.
-Ephesians 2:8-9

Grace is such a powerful word. Grace is God's unmerited favor bestowed upon all who will receive. The grace of God brings salvation to the world. We must humble ourselves and allow Christ to make intercession on our behalf through His precious blood. We could not pay the price for salvation. In our lost condition, our Father provided a Lamb, an acceptable sacrifice, in the form of His Son.

Christ's death on the cross provides the gift of grace needed for our atonement. We cannot work for our salvation. He offers His gift to all who will believe through faith. Our acceptance of His salvation is transforming and changes our lives forever. We are no longer concerned with our good works, but rather boast only in the work on cross.

Grace is sufficient. We have nothing to add to grace. Jesus' sacrifice on the cross fulfilled the law. Grace turns us to Christ to strengthen and grow us so that we may bear fruit. God's grace never leaves us. When we face difficult chapters in our life story, we need to lay hold of His sufficient grace. He provides all we need in salvation and will lead us through to eternal victory.

Grace gives us an everlasting heritage and provides us with hope. As sons and daughters of God, we are able to approach the Father through grace. No longer separated from Him, we have an advocate with the Father. He desires for us to come, and He will freely distribute mercy. The Father knows us intimately and bestows favor in our hour of need.

The seed of grace planted into the life of another yields hope, mercy, favor, and most importantly, the free gift of salvation. Today is the day to plant seeds of God's grace in the lives of others. It will not return void.

Sowing the Seeds

Grace has the ability to put your life into perspective. When you stop to think about the grace God shown to you when He sent His Son to die on the cross, you will find yourself more humble. In this humbled state, you are more willingly to sow grace into the lives of others. Thank Him for the completed work of the cross. Because of this work, we can boldly approach the Father's throne in our time of need.

Seeds of Change Prayer

Jesus, when I am discouraged in life, remind me that Your grace is all that I need. You have paid for my sin. You promise an everlasting heritage in Heaven. Help me to sow seeds of grace into others. These seeds will yield the treasure of hope in all who allow them to take root.

Tammy L Jordan

First Fruits

Record how God is instructing you to sow Seeds of Grace
and list what fruit it produces.

_____

_____

_____

_____

_____

_____

_____

_____

_____

_____

_____

_____

_____

_____

_____

_____

*For by grace are ye saved through faith; and that not of
yourselves: it is the gift of God:
Not of works, lest any man should boast.*
-Ephesians 2:8-9

Day 29: Sow Seeds of Longsuffering

But thou, O Lord, [art] a God full of compassion, and gracious, longsuffering, and plenteous in mercy and truth.

-Psalms 86:15

It is sometimes difficult to understand God's ways. How can a just and perfect God have such compassion on a fallen race? We betray Him, mock Him, deny Him, and refuse to share His love with others. The Father's compassion is too much for us to comprehend. He sent His only Son to be bruised for our transgressions so that He could extend the gift of grace to every person. No one is too sinful to accept the blessing of salvation. The longsuffering of God shines through this act of forgiveness. He knew before the foundation of time and before the creation of man, that a sin sacrifice was needed for man's redemption. Knowing the sacrifice that would be required, He still created man for His pleasure. Today Jesus stands patiently waiting on us to open our hearts to Him. Once we accept His gift of salvation, His longsuffering continues to flow forth. He still waits in times of our failure so that He can restore our precious relationship.

As we consider how forgiving the Father is to each of us, from the worst sinner to the best saint, how much more do we need to show longsuffering? It is so easy to feel the sting of betrayal and allow seeds of bitterness to take root in our heart. We may encounter those who mock our faith, question our devotion to Christ, or say our ways are for the weak-minded. Some may even claim there is no God. We must suffer long and show great mercy to those who seek to hurt us with their words. We are their light in a dark world. It is important to show the compassion that God showers so freely over our life.

Our walk, our testimony, needs to reflect our Savior's reaction to difficulties. We need to sow a different seed than the world is accustomed to encountering. It is easy to get into a rut of instant gratification. This is especially true in a defensive situation. However, as a Christian we are to sow seeds of change. This seed of longsuffering does bear the weight of suffering for Christ. Longsuffering calls us to wait for His timing. We need to decide to endure, to be steadfast, consistent in the ways of Christ, and slow to take vengeance. It is important to sow the beautiful seed of longsuffering generously. A change we cannot imagine will take place in our lives and the lives of those who have this seed take root in their heart.

Sowing the Seeds

Forgive someone who hurt you. Willingly sow the seed of longsuffering into their life. You will be surprised at the burden this lifts from you. Being obedient to wait for God's timing is another step to living out the full plans God has for you. By remembering the sacrifices Jesus made for you, it becomes easier to bless others with the seed of longsuffering.

Seeds of Change Prayer

Lord, teach me your ways. May my life be full of mercy and truth. When others entice me to respond to their negative actions, help me to follow Your leading and respond with longsuffering. Allow that precious seed to take root and grow in a world that often needs to first see a change in me in order to believe in You.

First Fruits

Record how God is instructing you to sow Seeds of
Longsuffering
and list what fruit it produces.

_____

_____

_____

_____

_____

_____

_____

_____

_____

_____

_____

_____

_____

_____

*But thou, O Lord, [art] a God full of compassion, and gracious,
longsuffering, and plenteous in mercy and truth.*
-Psalms 86:15

Day 30: Sow Seeds of Virtue

Finally; brethren, whatsoever things are true,
whatsoever things are honest, whatsoever things
are just, whatsoever things are pure, whatsoever
things are lovely, whatsoever things are of good
report; if there be any virtue, and if there be any
praise, think on these things.

-Philippians 4:8

Virtue dictates the way we live our life. We can better understand the depth of living an honorable life when we look deeply into the private recesses of our heart. Living virtuously leads to public actions, which reflect the same excellence as our thoughts. God understands that it is difficult to control our private thoughts. For this reason He gives us detailed instructions in His Word. Our Father knows that the heart of the virtuous believer dwells on things that are true, honest, just, pure, lovely, and of good report. Dwelling on the good things makes it easier to live a virtuous life. Today's thoughts are tomorrow's actions. If we continuously think on good, wholesome things, then our actions start to emulate these positive ways.

When we continue to meditate upon things that reflect the traits of God, it is easy to see how these thoughts translate into a life of virtue. Our expressions become more pure, honest, and true. We understand heavenly justice differs from worldly justification for our desired actions. Good reports flow forth from our mouths and degrading hurtful words cease. This change does not happen in a day. It takes time. God provided the blueprint of how to achieve this type of virtuous living.

As a new believer, we begin our first steps by faith. Our knowledge increases as we dig into His Word. His Word trains us to restrain our fleshly nature. Using self-control teaches us to be patient with ourselves and with others. As patience develops, it allows us to reflect on how God responds to situations. When we allow God to show us His plans, and we wait upon Him to develop those plans in our life, it leads to godliness. His plans will reveal ways we need to sow into the lives of others. Brotherly kindness takes root and out of it grows the love of God. Where we were once barren, seeds of virtue develop, and allow us to become fruitful.

Sowing the Seeds

God has given you a blueprint for virtuous living. The first step is living by faith. Daily practice using your faith, and watching how God increases your ability to rely on Him grows a deeper relationship with God. He will begin to increase His work in your life. As you follow His voice and His Word, you draw closer to Him. Growth allows you to begin comparing yourself to His reflection and that realization promotes change. Take time to thank God for teaching and mentoring you as you sow seeds of virtue.

Seeds of Change Prayer

Lord, please give me the strength that I need to follow Your exact plan on how to become more fruitful. Help me surrender my thoughts to Your thoughts. When I think upon things that are true, honest, and just, You are able to teach me a virtuous lifestyle. As You work in my life, I'll be able to grow and share Your path with others.

First Fruits

Record how God is instructing you to sow Seeds of Virtue
and list what fruit it produces.

_____

_____

_____

_____

_____

_____

_____

_____

_____

_____

_____

_____

*Finally, brethren, whatsoever things are true, whatsoever things
are honest, whatsoever things are just, whatsoever things are
pure, whatsoever things are lovely, whatsoever things are of good
report; if there be any virtue, and if there be any praise,
think on these things.*
-Philippians 4:8

Day 31: Sow Seeds of Faith

*So then faith cometh by hearing, and hearing by
the Word of God.*

-Romans 10:17

Two types of faith commonly surround the miracle of
Jesus. Those two types are great faith and little faith. We
know that faith comes by hearing. What do we need to hear to
receive faith? To believe by faith, we must first hear and accept
the Word of God. God has a very clear plan of salvation. It is
necessary to take the first step of faith to believe. We can do
nothing in our own strength, but rather we simply accept
salvation as the gift of God.

Acceptance of salvation allows our faith to develop. Each
believer's level of faith depends upon how much trust that
believer can place in God. Some believers will have great faith,
and others will have little faith. As trust levels increase, seeds
of faith begin to grow.

When we explore the miracles performed by Jesus while
He was on earth, we clearly see faith rewarded and lack of faith
rebuked. Having great faith usually resulted in great healing.
Having little faith resulted in His chastisement. This approach
promoted growth in the lives of new Christians. The apostles
heard His rebuke, but still experienced the miracle of having
the storm calmed while in the boat with Christ. His rebuke may
seem harsh, because each of these men had abandoned
everything to follow Christ; however, He used every word to
mold them into disciples strong enough to endure the
persecutions of the early church. We too need to be shaped in
our Christian walk in order to believe that all things are
possible with God. He can move mountains on our behalf, and
we can transition into a life of greater faith.

Great faith lets God work at His best. No strings
attached. This type of faith prompted a Roman centurion to
come on behalf of his servant who needed healing. He
proclaimed that one word from Jesus would heal his servant.
Jesus responded with a miracle and a beautiful passage of
praise for the man's faith. Many other accounts reflect great

faith such as the healing of the man with palsy, the blind being healed, and the woman with a blood disease that touched the hem of Christ's garment. Healing and encouragement come when Jesus encounters great faith. After being made whole, the believer departs in peace. It is important for us as believers to learn to walk by faith. The results are always transforming.

Sowing the Seeds

Do you have great faith or little faith? One way to increase your faith is to meditate on past success. Think about a time when you had little faith. How did God work in your situation? Share your testimony with other believers so that you can be encouraged as well as giving encouragement. This will allow you to grow in faith together.

Seeds of Change Prayer

Father, I desire to lay aside little faith in exchange for great faith. Just as the apostles, I need You to increase my faith. I understand that, to increase faith, I may encounter difficulties ahead. It is worth these challenges, because along the way I am able to watch You move mountains on my behalf. In the end, You will have my fully surrendered life to work through. I pray that others will see these seeds of faith pushing up through the soil of disbelief, and it will allow their faith to increase.

First Fruits

Record how God is instructing you to sow Seeds of Faith
and list what fruit it produces.

_____

_____

_____

_____

_____

_____

_____

_____

_____

_____

_____

_____

_____

_____

_____

_____

_____

_____

_____

So then faith cometh by hearing, and hearing by the Word of God.
-Romans 10:17

Day 32: Sow Seeds of Patience

And not only [so], but we glory in tribulations also: knowing that tribulation worketh patience; And patience, experience; and experience, hope: And hope maketh not ashamed; because the love of God is shed abroad in our hearts by the Holy Ghost which is given unto us.

-Romans 5:3-5

It is hard to understand that as a believer, we should glory, or count, tribulations and difficulties as joy. Yet when we explore the ways of Christ, we understand that difficulties are ultimately the path to sharing the love of God. Significant growth takes place during seasons of trials and tribulations. When things in life are progressing as planned, we just hold steady to the course. We like the rhythm of calmness. However, when storms enter into the equation, God's leading takes us from tribulations to hope. It just takes time.

Picture a difficult day. Now picture a difficult day extending into a difficult week, then a difficult month, and maybe even a difficult year. Our minds usually race to a very specific series of trials. As the storm passes through ever so slowly, we start to change. Seeing that the storm is not going to end quickly, we accept that this is the place God has us for a reason. While we may not understand it, a weariness of body and soul demand we learn the sustaining principle of waiting on Him. In this undetermined period of endurance, God begins molding our ways to His ways. We learn that steadfastness in our faith helps make the journey easier. This faith teaches us to be patient. Waiting upon His plans brings about a better result than rushing ahead.

As we patiently wait for God to deliver us, the experience is, at times, overwhelming and sometimes it tries our character. It presses us beyond our limits and into our Father's strength. Resting in Him refines what we think and do in private. Instead of appearing to rest our faith in Him, we actually learn to give it all to Him. As we lay the weight at His feet, we surrender our will to God's way. What happens next in our heart is similar to taking a refreshing breath of air after a delightful summer rain. When our character shifts to His design, God can flood us with hope. With Him leading us, all things are now possible! When He delivers us, we are no longer ashamed to share His hope and love to all we meet. Without first encountering trials, we can never have seeds of patience planted into our life.

Sowing the Seeds

Glory in tribulation is a phrase that does not make sense. However, that is exactly what God instructs you to do. God certainly understands the pain of the trial, but, more importantly, he understands the outcome of the trial. Give God thanks for your trial today and sow seeds of patience.

Seeds of Change Prayer

Lord, when I am facing tribulations, help me to embrace patience. Let me run the race that is set before me. Plant deeply into my soul the desire to continue on whatever path You prepare. Father, I now understand that sowing seeds of patience yields the fruit of hope.

Tammy L Jordan

First Fruits

Record how God is instructing you to sow Seeds of Patience
and list what fruit it produces.

_____

_____

_____

_____

_____

_____

_____

_____

_____

_____

_____

_____

_____

And not only [so], but we glory in tribulations also: knowing that tribulation worketh patience; And patience, experience; and experience, hope: And hope maketh not ashamed; because the love of God is shed abroad in our hearts by the Holy Ghost which is given unto us.
-Romans 5:3-5

Part 5: Wholeness Seeds

Salvation
Hope
Joy
Forgiveness
Restoration
Healing
Purpose
Surrender

Day 33: Sow Seeds of Salvation

The LORD [is] my light and my salvation; whom shall I fear? the LORD [is] the strength of my life; of whom shall I be afraid?

-Psalms 27:1

Sometimes, just as it seems all hope is gone, God plants a seed in our life that reminds us He is our light and our salvation. Just as light pierces even the darkest valley, salvation reaches the very recesses of our heart. This light provides visibility to our sin and warmth in the emptiness of life. When we accept God's salvation, it fills a void inside of us that no other possession, pleasure, or person can fill. We no longer have to seek out distractions, addictions, or relationships for temporary satisfaction. Salvation brings something to our life that nothing else is capable of endlessly supplying. It brings hope!

When we allow the seeds of salvation to grow in our heart, we do things that reach beyond our past actions. The Lord becomes the strength in our life. As we place our trust in His strength, He removes the pressure of fear that often holds us back from doing things for Him.

Salvation is an exciting journey. It takes us to the door to fruitfulness, where God's plans for our life come alive. The path is not always easy, but the results are a freedom that we have never encountered. When we place our trust in Him, He is able to set aside fear from our mind, open doors we would normally be afraid to enter, and use us to show His love to a world of others that need the seed of salvation sown into their life.

Sowing the Seeds

You are standing at the door to fruitfulness. Your success depends on how you apply the knowledge He is growing in your life. Allow His light to shine in the dark places in your life. As those places are filled with His light, His plan for you will come alive. Bask in His light. Enjoy the warmth that only salvation can bring. As your heart is filled with His love, share that love with others so that the gospel can be shared with a hurting world. Sow seeds of salvation today.

Seeds of Change Prayer

Lord, once I receive Your gift of salvation, I'm able to call You Father. You become my light and my strength. Give me the courage I need to follow the plan You have for me, so that I'm able to share the precious seed of the gospel to those who need to hear of Your great love.

First Fruits

Record how God is instructing you to sow Seeds of Salvation
and list what fruit it produces.

_____

_____

_____

_____

_____

_____

_____

_____

_____

_____

_____

_____

_____

_____

_____

*The LORD [is] my light and my salvation; whom shall I fear? the LORD [is] the
strength of my life; of whom shall I be afraid?*
-Psalms 27:1

Day 34: Sow Seeds of Hope

Hope deferred maketh the heart sick: but [when]
the desire cometh, [it is] a tree of life.

-Proverbs 13:12

We hope for many things in life. Sometimes, we hope for simple things such as rain to stop, vacation to start, or appreciation for our labors. Hopes for those things are fleeting, and at the end of the day, they are not important. We quickly forget and move forward. However, there is another type of hope. It is a hope so powerful that when it is delayed it makes the heart sick.

Deferred hope is a deep hope invested in things that forever change the course of life. Maybe it is the illness of a child or spouse. Our hope desires healing. When that healing is postponed, we often experience deep emotional distress. Other types of delayed hopes are waiting for a marriage to be restored, huge financial pressures to be relieved, employment to be acquired after a long period of unemployment, a family member's murder to be solved, or a child to be found after getting lost in the woods.

We often wait for years for these types of situations to be resolved. The resolution changes our life in a powerful way. Weights lift from our hearts, and we feel blessed. Deliverance yields abundant praise to our Father. The Father, in turn, allows the seed of hope to grow into a tree of life. When necessary, He will use fellow believers to nurture this seed through difficult seasons. For this reason, it is important to speak words of peace and encouragement into the lives of others when hope has been deferred.

Sowing the Seeds

Sow the seed of hope today. We all know someone whose hope has been deferred. God will give you a word for their situation. When this happens, don't be afraid to share what God has laid on your heart. The word God gives you may just be the very thing that encourages them to hold on to see their promise fulfilled.

Seeds of Change Prayer

Lord, allow hope to reside in my life, especially when it has been delayed. Help my heart to continue to rest in You during lengthy seasons of distress. I understand that I will grow weary waiting for answers that could alter the course of life. However, I take comfort in knowing that no matter how long I must wait for resolution, You are right there beside of me. All I have to do is lean into You. You will send others to nurture that small seed of hope that remains, and continue to help it grow inside of me. I will rejoice when the matured seed of hope, develops into a tree of life. May I use this tree to draw many people to see Your great and mighty works.

First Fruits

Record how God is instructing you to sow Seeds of Hope
and list what fruit it produces.

_____

_____

_____

_____

_____

_____

_____

_____

_____

_____

_____

_____

_____

_____

_____

_____

Hope deferred maketh the heart sick; but [when] *the desire cometh,*
[it is] *a tree of life.*
-Proverbs 13:12

Day 35: Sow Seeds of Joy

...weeping may endure for a night, but joy
[cometh] *in the morning.*

-Psalms 30:5

There are many joys in life. Some joys are small joys, such as the start of spring each year after a long snowy winter, and others are great joys like the birth of your first child. Each joy has the possibility of being stolen. Rain may set in after that first lovely spring day, and sleepless nights are often the theme of new parenthood. Joy may also slip away from us due to our own poor choices. It is up to us to capture joy, so that it remains though all circumstances. Happiness is rooted in circumstances, but joy abides.

It is hard to believe, but we allow temporary discouragements to steal precious simple joys. We may even permit those discouragements to rob us of the joy found in our salvation. When life circumstances change, service for the Father can become difficult. Our energy levels deplete and the storm sets in for what seems like months of endless nights.

When our joy levels are running close to empty, we often find our heart weary and ready to faint. The desire to give up becomes stronger with each passing day. "Why bother?" This negative response seems to be the answer to every question about why we don't change something to get us out of our negative spiral. In scripture, our loving Father reminds us that weeping and sorrow will last through our night, but when morning dawns on a new day, it brings joy.

We must keep moving forward with Him to keep from planting our roots in the discouragement of the night. God desires to see a new day dawn in our life, and joy to come. Living in the past limits His ability to change our future. Moving forward is not an easy task, especially in the middle of some of life's largest storms. It is like trying to move a heavy object on wheels. The first few pushes takes almost all of our energy to barely inch forward, but then once the wheels start turning, we are able move farther away from our starting point with less effort. Focusing on joy is similar. When facing trials or recovering from poor choices on our part, it requires great effort to think positively. Often we must start by focusing on the joy of salvation. Then we begin counting our blessings. As we push farther away from discouragement, we move with increasing momentum towards joy. God leads on this journey. He even provides other believers to help plant seeds of joy in our heart with thoughtful actions and words. Moving forward in joy is a learned behavior.

Sowing the Seeds

Learn to focus each day on what God has done in your life. Surround yourself with believers who exhibit great joy. You will find their joy contagious. Slowly, but surely you will step into that new day full of new joy. Learn to walk daily in joy.

Seeds of Change Prayer

Lord, as the weights of life continue to pull at me, and I feel my heart becoming faint and weary, please help me to run to You for restoration of joy. Without abiding in joy, it is easy for me to slip into the routine of negative thoughts and remain in the darkness. You desire to bring me through the storm, and to allow me to pass through the valley while claiming joy in my salvation. This one simple act of retaining joy in difficulties sows seeds of life into those who encounter Your joy in me.

Tammy L Jordan

First Fruits

Record how God is instructing you to sow Seeds of Joy
and list what fruit it produces.

_____

_____

_____

_____

_____

_____

_____

_____

_____

_____

_____

_____

_____

_____

_____

_____

_____

...weeping may endure for a night, but joy [cometh] *in the morning.*
-Psalms 30:5

Day 36: Sow Seeds of Forgiveness

If we confess our sins, he is faithful and just to forgive us [our] sins, and to cleanse us from all unrighteousness.

-1 John 1:9

Forgiving another for inflicting deep pain upon our life is a difficult task. Sometimes it is even a challenge to forgive petty arguments. The Apostle Peter asked how many times he should forgive another, and Jesus responded, "...seventy times seven". In other words, we should always have a forgiving spirit. This does not mean, though, that we should be a doormat and let others run over us. Rather, when someone comes to us and seeks true forgiveness, we should be willing to forgive. Forgiving another person has a great benefit for us, as well: relationships are restored and weights lift from both sides. We must always remember that we are not perfect and will need to seek forgiveness of others. How can we expect someone to pardon our shortcomings, if we are not willing to forgive others?

Maybe we find ourselves in a different situation, where we are the ones that need forgiveness. We have the assurance that God will forgive our sins. This challenging place separates us from a fulfilling relationship with our Father unless we are willing to confess our sin before God.

Many times, we decide to ignore our sin, justify our sin, or we blame it on another. Instead, we should simply follow the Lord's plan for forgiveness. "If my people, which are called by my name, shall humble themselves, and pray, and seek my face, and turn from their wicked ways; then will I hear from heaven, and will forgive their sin, and will heal their land."

Sowing the Seeds

When God reveals the sin in your life, you must humble yourself before a Holy God. It is important to escape the desire to ignore, justify, or blame another for the sin. In humility, seek God's face through a devoted time of prayer, where He is able to speak about this sin situation. After this prayer of private confession with God, He will provide the strength to turn completely from this sinful act. Forgiveness is offered, and the healing of the relationship follows. Remember, when God forgives the sins against Him, and against your own flesh, you need to then forgive yourself. The act of forgiving oneself is a part of complete healing and returning to a place of wholeness.

Seeds of Change Prayer

Father, help me to refrain from intentionally harming another person. When this occurs, allow my heart to be sensitive and ask for forgiveness as soon as this hurt is revealed. Lord, may I likewise be ready to sow seeds of forgiveness when someone comes and seeks it. I'm reminded of the healing that occurs when we open up to another and share the benefits of forgiveness. Even for the ones that never come to ask forgiveness, give me the strength to still forgive and not hold a grudge against them. Most importantly, show me where I have sinned against You, so that I may humble myself and allow restoration of our relationship to take place.

First Fruits

Record how God is instructing you to sow Seeds of Forgiveness
and list what fruit it produces.

_____

_____

_____

_____

_____

_____

_____

_____

_____

_____

_____

_____

_____

_____

_____

_____

*If we confess our sins, he is faithful and just to forgive us [our] sins,
and to cleanse us from all unrighteousness.*
-1 John 1:9

Day 37: Sow Seeds of Restoration

Brethren, if a man be overtaken in a fault, ye which are spiritual, restore such an one in the spirit of meekness; considering thyself, lest thou also be tempted. Bear ye one another's burdens, and so fulfil the law of Christ.

-Galatians 6:1-2

It is much easier to complain or gossip about someone who has lost direction in life than it is to reach out to help. Intervention on behalf of another who is experiencing a downward spiral is not an easy or pleasant task. However, the results may be life altering for both parties.

Restoration is a delicate path to walk. When thinking about the concept of restoring another person, we can compare it to the process of restoring a piece of furniture. Usually this piece, covered with undesirable paint, is rough and weathered. The skilled carpenter first removes all the hardware and takes each piece apart one at a time. Next, starts the painfully slow process of stripping off the old paint layer by layer. Salvaging something others no longer value takes great care and compassion. This process also requires skill and patience. Most cast it aside as rubbish. The carpenter, however, sees the potential and worth underneath all the layers of grime.

Restoration of a brother or sister in Christ mirrors the physical act of restoring furniture. It requires a mature, spiritual, and humble believer. In meekness, this believer approaches the one overtaken in a fault. Usually this distressed soul is hardened towards God and needs someone to gently remove the hard shell around their life. With that rigid armor of self-preservation removed, this gentle Christian slowly sifts through the layers of sin, undesirable actions, and rough lifestyle to the hidden precious soul. The process takes time and is not without frustration and much pain. This learned skill of restoration comes from many hours sitting at the Master's feet. The believer has learned to see others as Christ sees them. Underneath all the external wreckage there is a soul, which desires to shine. Out of the seed of restoration blooms a second chance full of potential.

Sowing the Seeds

Restoration is not always easy. In fact, it is usually messy. When you sow a restoration seed, you may get dirty. Not everyone will appreciate your effort to associate and restore that lost soul. You may face unexpected ridicule for wasting time and resources on this person many see as undesirable. Regardless, stand firm in seeing others through God's eyes and you can see the beauty of a life restored to God.

Seeds of Change Prayer

Father, help me grow spiritually, so that I might be the tool used to restore another's life. May I reflect Your spirit of meekness, and gently tend to the wounds of one overwhelmed in their sin. Lord, allow me to block out the noise of others that criticize this process and allow me to see this person through Your eyes. Please strengthen me so that I will always walk in Your ways. If sin enters into my life and derails Your plans, I pray that I will submit to the tender care of another one who desires to help restore me to You.

First Fruits

Record how God is instructing you to sow Seeds of Restoration and list what fruit it produces.

_____

_____

_____

_____

_____

_____

_____

_____

_____

_____

_____

_____

_____

_____

_____

_____

_____

Brethren, if a man be overtaken in a fault, ye which are spiritual, restore such an one in the spirit of meekness; considering thyself, lest thou also be tempted. Bear ye one another's burdens, and so fulfil the law of Christ.
-Galatians 6:1-2

Day 38: Sow Seeds of Healing

*But unto you that fear my name shall the Sun of
righteousness arise with healing in his wings;
and ye shall go forth...*

-Malachi 4:2

The word healing inspires such positive emotions.
When we hear the word healing, we generally think of physical
healing. However, while Jesus performed many physical
miracles, some of the greatest types of healing were not
physical ones. We rejoice when a fellow believer's battle with
cancer leads to physical remission, but the healing of God is so
much more than simply restoring health to this temporary shell
of a body. As believers, we understand that our flesh will not
live forever. In time, the body will wear out. The Father will
not endlessly heal our body. Life is fleeting, and like a vapor,
and our body has an appointment with death.

Thankfully, God does not limit healing to just the body.
We can rejoice as Christians that we can experience different
types of healing. The Bible says healing is in His wings for
those who fear Him. He comes and heals the brokenhearted,
the wounded of spirit, those with distressed souls, and most
importantly all who face spiritual sickness. These types of
healings are limited only by our willingness to receive it. His
wings extend to gather us unto Him for health and protection.
We must prepare for healing by submitting our broken heart to
Him. Our loving Father will determine when and how to wrap it
up with a healing balm.

So many times in our emotional distress, we decide to
bear the weight of brokenness alone, and wonder why God does
not heal us. It is important to understand that He has to
empty the exhausted and discouraged heart in order to fill and
restore it to health. Often, the emptying process seems to
worsen the health of our soul. We draw back and refuse to
complete the process or at least significantly delay it, causing
even greater pain in our life. It is not until we surrender to the
Master Physician's method of healing that the Father is given
freedom to fill and replenish.

The most significant form of healing is not of the body, mind, or soul, but of the spirit. Everyone stands in need of this healing in life, and it is free to whoever will receive it. This healing doesn't require a doctor or medicine, but it does require a payment that we cannot pay. This healing of sin sickness required the death of God's only Son on the cross. Jesus' atonement perpetually sows seeds of healing offered to all who desire it. As believers, may we always remember that His stripes, His blood, His death, and His resurrection heal us and prevent us from experiencing eternal death. Because of the importance of this spiritual healing, we must be willing to scatter seeds of healing liberally wherever we go. Eternal healing from the deathly disease of sin depends upon it.

Sowing the Seeds

Many times, as a child of the King, you are used to plant seeds of healing into the hearts and souls of others. These seeds are often words of encouragement. It is important that you are sensitive to His leading of sharing pleasant words with others. It may just be God's way of filling and replenishing health to a weary soul.

Seeds of Change Prayer

Father, I don't always understand why you do not heal others of sickness of body. Sometimes, I am especially sorrowful when a loved one passes into eternity, especially before I am ready. However, you lovingly remind me that our mortal bodies are not designed for eternity. It is important to accept the healing found in Your stripes so that the eternal spirit may forever dwell with You when this life ends. Help me to pray for the physical healing of others, knowing You are capable of supplying health to our bodies, but most importantly, may I sow seeds of eternal healing into the spirits of those still buried under the weight of sin.

First Fruits

Record how God is instructing you to sow Seeds of Healing
and list what fruit it produces.

_____

_____

_____

_____

_____

_____

_____

_____

_____

_____

_____

_____

_____

_____

_____

_____

_____

*But unto you that fear my name shall the Sun of righteousness arise
with healing in his wings; and ye shall go forth...*
-Malachi 4:2

Day 39: Sow Seeds of Purpose

And we know that all things work together for good to them that love God, to them who are the called according to [his] purpose.

-Romans 8:28

As believers, we certainly hope for all things in our life to work together for good. The biblical promise that all things work together comes with two requirements. We must love God and be called according to His purpose. We are all called to the same purpose, but He uses our unique gifts and talents to fulfill that purpose as individuals. The purpose of every believer is that salvation might be made known to the uttermost part of the world. It sounds simple, but it is difficult to apply this purpose in our daily walk.

Most believers (usually during difficult times) spend countless days seeking out God's purpose. It is easy to fall into the trap of wondering how things work together for good, while we refuse to take steps to learn of His specific purpose for our life. He does not withhold this purpose from us. Many of us are unwilling to follow Him on the journey to see how He desires to apply His eternal purpose in our life. When we find the courage to press forward, we follow Him to a simple door that will forever change our lives. We stand before the door to fruitfulness. The choice to enter rests in our control. God will not force us. While He has our full attention and devotion, He speaks and begins to reveal a purpose already placed in our heart.

Once we step beyond the door of fruitfulness our purpose unfolds. It may not be at a stage where we can share with others. In fact, at first, it is difficult to form a description of the desire He places in our hearts. In these early days of unveiling purpose, we need to continue to follow Him and allow things to just simply unfold. Our actions may seem odd to those around us. They might even question why we do certain things. Don't worry! This is a normal response to the early stages of this exciting journey.

As purpose unfolds in the life of a believer, God always places others in our path to give good counsel. They are there as mile markers to remind us that we are on the path He has planned. As we seek after His purpose for our life, fellow laborers will join us in the same vineyard. Seeking Godly counsel often opens these doors. God will overlap our paths in time and allow an even greater purpose to develop, as He forms support teams and detailed networks to encourage and strengthen one another. When God delivers others to us to help support the same purpose, we are able to rest in the fact that this purpose is of God, and not simply of our own desires. He will grow this purpose in our hearts and give a good reward for our labor.

The most difficult part about seeking purpose is waiting on God's timing. When we enter into the door to fruitfulness, we want to forge ahead with this new journey and see results immediately. Rest in knowing that He sees exactly where you are in life and knows how to move you beyond the open door of fruitfulness and into the labor of His vineyard.

Sowing the Seeds

Surround yourself with like-minded people. God will reveal to you those who share a common vision and purpose. Work together to develop the purpose God has for you. Don't get ahead of God. Allow Him to work His purpose in your life and then in turn you can sow seeds of purpose into others.

Seeds of Change Prayer

Father, I've followed You to the door to fruitfulness and I stand ready to take the next step. I know that You have revealed to my soul a unique way to fulfill my purpose for You. Give me the strength to endure ridicule from other believers who do not understand my actions. Help me to recognize others called to similar styles of purpose and allow me to lay aside any desire of full control or independence. Let us work as a team. Your Word promises a greater reward for our combined labors. Help us to give Godly advice when a fellow laborer is discouraged. May we quickly rush to strengthen one another. Finally, when I wish to run ahead of You, give me the discernment I desperately need to wait patiently upon Your leading.

First Fruits

Record how God is instructing you to sow Seeds of Purpose
and list what fruit it produces.

_____

_____

_____

_____

_____

_____

_____

_____

_____

_____

_____

_____

_____

_____

_____

_____

And we know that all things work together for good to them that love God,
to them who are the called according to [his] purpose.
-Romans 8:28

Day 40: Sow Seeds of Surrender

And be not conformed to this world: but be ye transformed by the renewing of your mind, that ye may prove what [is] that good, and acceptable, and perfect, will of God.

-Romans 12:2

Surrender comes with a seemingly great price. Initially, surrendering to God's requests does not feel it is worth the cost. Sometimes, He asks us to lay aside things that we treasure the most to come and follow Him. When we read the accounts of Christ's time here on earth, we encounter three different types of people that were interested in His ministry. Some followed for what He could offer to them. When He departed, they too departed in a separate way. Others came to inquire of His ways, but were unwilling to forego the things requested to embrace the life He promised. Then we see those who were willing to give up all they had, even their lives, to follow the Savior.

God's teaching says that we should be willing to offer up our life unto His hands, and this is just our reasonable service. It is not an extraordinary offering compared to what Jesus gave on the cross. When we give our bodies as a living sacrifice, it means that we are willing to seek God's will for our life regardless of the initial cost. To do anything less is unacceptable to the Father. God understands that it is against our nature to surrender everything to Him. He is patient as we learn and mature in His ways.

As immature believers, we often desire to live one foot in the world and one foot at the cross. It is easy to seek what is appealing in both worlds. The Father sees how detrimental this is to our overall growth. When the will of God takes root in a surrendered life, it transforms the entire individual. Many times people may even remark about the outward glow of a person who is following God's will. The transformation and renewing of the mind leads us to align our will with the Father's plan. We surrender all we have to follow Christ. We focus completely on Him. Any other path away from God is considered a path of great loss. The act of placing all that we treasure and hold dear at the feet of Jesus allows us to develop a lifelong journey that is good and acceptable to God. It leads us to maturity and completeness in Him. Seeds of surrender develop into lives that are whole and pure in thought and deed.

Sowing the Seeds

Surrender is not easy, yet it is important to surrender to His plan for your life. Allow Him to mold and shape you into the believer He wants you to be. Avoid being double-minded. Don't try to please God and man. Surrender your life to God as a living sacrifice.

Seeds of Change Prayer

It is difficult to surrender my life to You with faith that You will transform it. I often desire to change it on my own to make it better, but my ways end in a lesser plan. Father, I believe now is the time to enter into Your ways. I surrender all of myself to the path of Your good, acceptable, and perfect will. As I grow and develop in the plans You have for me, help me to sow seeds of surrender into the lives of others, so they too will receive the joy found in a surrendered life.

Record how God is instructing you to sow Seeds of Surrender
and list what fruit it produces.

_____

_____

_____

_____

_____

_____

_____

_____

_____

_____

_____

_____

_____

_____

_____

And be not conformed to this world:
but be ye transformed by the renewing of your mind,
that ye may prove what [is] that good, and acceptable, and perfect, will of God.
-Romans 12:2

Conclusion

Our focus with this forty-day journey is sowing into the lives of others around us. During this season of sowing, we may have been called to sow into those we know and love, complete strangers, or maybe even into the lives of our enemies. The seeds sown during this planting period may have been sown at a small cost or with great sacrifice. The hope is that the sower no longer counts the cost. We may never fully see how God uses these small seeds to reap a great harvest in His vineyard. As we move forward sowing into the lives of others, let us never fail to also be open to God sowing into us.

As we complete this journey, we have a very important seed we must sow daily. This seed is sown into our own life. "Sow to yourselves in righteousness, reap in mercy; break up your fallow ground: for [it is] time to seek the LORD, till he come and rain righteousness upon you" (Hosea 10:12). God reveals to each of us how to continuously sow His righteousness into our lives so that we may reap in mercy. When we seek after His ways, the Father teaches us to submit our lives to Him. It is important to allow the Master Gardener to expand His vineyard in us by breaking up and cultivating our fallow ground. This process may not always feel great. Just as a plow loosens the soil, God sometimes must loosen our grip on things of this world. Little by little, we may watch as precious dreams slip through our hands. In disbelief, we may question His ways, yet it is important to continue sowing seeds into the freshly tilled earth. In time, the Father will come and rain righteousness down upon our lives. This rain allows fruit to grow and be gathered in the season of harvest!

Empty Hands

by Tammy Jordan

It is in the darkness that I cry out to You.
It is in the night that I whisper Your name in silence.
I feel You have left me alone.
And yet it is I that stops and stands still out of fear.

My heart knows not the passing of time.
How many days, weeks, months have I stood still?
In the middle of weakness I sink to my knees.
My heart is so heavy that the only thing heard is a groan.

I breathe in only a shallow breath,
For the weight of despair resides in my soul.
I sing not songs of glory and praise,
Rather distress is falling from my lips.

In a human attempt to reason with God I simply say, "Why me?"
In love my Father says, "Because it is My way for you."
I watch my dreams slip through clasped hands,
And He says, "Have faith and open your palms to me."

Closing them tighter as if to salvage something I wait...
I wait until all has slipped through, and then I open to reveal emptiness.
I open my hands to say, "Why did You not restore as I have poured out to You in prayer?"
I open them to say, "Why did You not help me hold onto the dreams that were realized?"

The Father waits as I lament over the loss of the dreams built out of my sorrow.
Slowly, He takes my empty hands and says, "I must have them empty."
I question, "Why? Why must they be empty?" as I fully extend my exhausted hands.
Patiently, my Father says, "I wish to fill them with dreams borne out of My joy."

"There are plans, dreams, and blessings that I have prepared for you,
But to receive them you must first have empty hands."

About the Author

Growing up in the beautiful, lush mountains of West Virginia, **Tammy L. Jordan** has always had a deep love for nature. At

the age of five, she dreamed of owning a farm, and that desire only grew with time. After many years of working in agricultural research, Tammy stepped out by faith and went full time with her company Fruits of Labor, Inc., which marries agriculture with culinary arts. The company expanded into retreat-style ministry with the purchase of the 218-acre Fruits of Labor Training & Retreat Center.

The Retreat Center offers women's retreats, special interest day retreats, and the Training Center is scheduled to offer a new culinary and agricultural program for recovering addicts beginning the summer of 2013. Tammy's next books *The Seed Sower* and *Seeds of Recovery* are slated to be released Fall 2013. Tammy Jordan is launching a non-profit sister company called Seed Sower Inc. in the spring of 2014 to assist in the ministry and outreach side of the organization. Please visit www.fruitsoflaborinc.com to learn more about retreat opportunities and training programs. Tammy's desire to become more fruitful for God has become her priority in life.

Author's Acknowledgements

To my Heavenly Father, who never fails to inspire my heart when I sit silently with Him opening my mind, and surrendered to seeking His purpose. He has never failed to provide all that I need to move ahead with His plans for me.

To Fruits of Labor's Vision Counselor Team: Dawn, Debbie, Dora, Dyanna, India, Jennifer, Johnetta, and Linda, who experienced the Seed Sowing journey with me as it was being written. Each of you provided endless inspiration, encouragement, and great wisdom! Thank you for believing in and laboring with this ministry!

To ShadeTree Publishing: Jennifer, your endless excitement and words of truth provide an environment where God can work through you in powerful ways! I'm so thankful He has called us to labor during this season, in the same section of His vineyard.

To Steve Brightwell: My dear friend and an extremely talented photographer, thank you for the gift of the cover picture and author picture. Words cannot express how thankful I am for your willingness to be part of *The Seed Sower*.

To Kathy Lawrence: Thank you for your behind-the-scenes labor with additional editing and rewrites. Your talent and willingness to be a part of this project is cherished.

To my parents: Whose teaching and example sowed into me seeds of wholeness. For your sacrificial investment of sowing endlessly into my life, and this outreach ministry, I am forever grateful. I endlessly praise God for the treasure and support system He has given to me in the two of you!

To my brother Kevin, his wife Beth, and my precious nephew Cayden: Thank you for believing so much in this ministry. It is with excitement, we embark upon a lifelong experience together of sowing precious seed with this ministry. We know the journey ahead may be as difficult as it is rewarding, and through it all, our lives will forever be changed!

And finally to my Godly husband, Derek: Whose rich supply of seeds of kindness, faith, and love are sown deeply into my life every day. Your love fills me endlessly with great joy, peace, and hope!

Fruits of Labor is where the fruit of the earth meets the fruit of the Spirit. The training and retreat center is designed as a place of sustainability in agricultural practices, lifestyle principles, and spiritual growth for longevity of service.

> *Come experience a setting where agricultural research, culinary passion, and hospitality coincide with training programs and renewal retreats.*

Fruits of Labor is dedicated to providing a mountaintop experience that prepares individuals with education, experience, and training in agriculture, culinary, and hospitality industries. At *Fruits of Labor*, we grow much of our own fruits and vegetables used to prepare mouth-watering meals for retreat guests seeking to rejuvenate and draw away from the hectic pace of their spiritual ministries.

The retreat center, situated on 218 acres of land at over 3200 feet in elevation, will surround the mind, body, and spirit with a peaceful, natural environment. Walking trails, gardens, and other recreational activities are available. The retreat center offers serene accommodations with private meditation areas and beautiful vistas to enhance the experience.

Types of Training and Retreats:

- Pastor/Pastor Couples Retreats ~ Come, and allow God to renew, restore, heal, and re-energize your ministries. We have scholarship opportunities available for pastors.
- Restoration Retreats ~ Various retreats are available throughout the year to help strengthen the church body and family. Healthy churches, first start with healthy individual Christians who are motivated to pray, serve, and labor.
- Leadership Retreats ~ Leadership retreats help individuals and groups draw away from the normal hectic pace of life, find time to relax, and let their mind open to new ideas and concepts.
- Culinary and Agricultural Training Program ~ This training program is specially designed for recovering addicts. The program works with the whole person, and offers training in the culinary industry and farm-to-table movement to help increase job opportunities.

To learn more about *Fruits of Labor*, schedule a retreat, or make a donation towards one of the programs, please contact Tammy Jordan at fruitsoflaborinc@hotmail.com or visit our website at www.fruitsoflaborinc.com.

About the First Fruit Series

The *First Fruit Series* is designed to bring honor to the Lord and is based upon the principles found in Proverbs 3:9.

> *Honour the Lord with thy substance, and with the firstfruits of all thine increase.*

Bearing First Fruits is a unique and wonderful part of the Christian experience that grows out of surrendering our will to God's will for our life. The key ingredient to bearing First Fruits is to set our heart towards God and become willing to allow His hands to shape us.

The *First Fruits Series* walks us through the lifelong cycle from the first step of seeking God's will all the way to the harvest season. It comprises multiple books to meet us wherever we are along the path.

- *The Door to Fruitfulness* is for those desiring to produce more for the Lord, but finding themselves inundated with unproductive busyness and unable to find a starting point. It is a map to the door of the Master Gardener's vineyard.
- *Beyond the Open Door* is for those who have actively crossed over into the Lord's vineyard and

entered a place of God's vision for their life. It teaches how to lean on Him and see the world through His eyes.

- *The Seed Sower* is for those ready to go deeper and harvest more. It reveals how to produce fruit by sowing into the lives of others.
- *Seeds of Recovery* is a special training program that encourages participants to reach beyond themselves to embrace the needs of others. It deals with addiction issues and uses compassion and service for others as a method of recovery.

If you find your lips whispering the sweet prayer of surrender, "Lord, use me as You see fit", but need inspiration to step forward or desire comfort while waiting for His leading, the *First Fruit Series* is for you. It meets you where you are in your walk with Christ and encourages you for the journey of fruit bearing ahead.

Tammy L Jordan